Twenty questions
Jesus asked
What is he asking you?

Text copyright © Elizabeth Rundle 2008
The author asserts the moral right
to be identified as the author of this work

Published by
The Bible Reading Fellowship
15 The Chambers, Vineyard
Abingdon OX14 3FE
United Kingdom
Tel: +44 (0)1865 319700
Email: enquiries@brf.org.uk
Website: www.brf.org.uk

ISBN 978 1 84101 568 2
First published 2008
10 9 8 7 6 5 4 3 2 1 0
All rights reserved

Acknowledgments
Unless otherwise stated, scripture quotations are taken from the Holy Bible, New
International Version, copyright © 1973, 1978, 1984 by International Bible Society, and
are used by permission of Hodder & Stoughton Publishers, a division of Hodder
Headline Ltd. All rights reserved. 'NIV' is a registered trademark of International Bible
Society. UK trademark number 1448790.

Scripture quotations from The New Revised Standard Version of the Bible, Anglicized
Edition, copyright © 1989, 1995 by the Division of Christian Education of the National
Council of the Churches of Christ in the United States of America, are used by
permission. All rights reserved.

Extracts from the Authorized Version of the Bible (The King James Bible), the rights in
which are vested in the Crown, are reproduced by permission of the Crown's Patentee,
Cambridge University Press.

A catalogue record for this book is available from the British Library

Printed in Singapore by Craft Print International Ltd

Twenty questions
Jesus asked
What is he asking you?

Elizabeth Rundle

Acknowledgments

My thanks to Naomi Starkey, Lisa Cherrett and Linda Chester
for their suggestions, attention to detail and encouragement
as this book has taken shape.

Contents

(handwritten margin notes: "25/11" alongside Chapters 1–2; "2/12" alongside Chapters 3–4; "9/12" alongside Chapter 14; "16/12" alongside Chapter 15; "16/12" alongside Chapter 17)

Introduction

Sitting on the back row in the classroom, I was under the (mistaken) impression that the teacher wouldn't ask me any questions. Others in the class seemed only too eager to wave their hands in the air, straining to show their knowledge, but I was seldom confident that my answer would be correct.

Years later, as a member of the local Young Wives group, I ended up on the team for the annual quiz night, when we pitted our wits against half a dozen other local teams. A wretched question was put to me which has burnt itself into my memory: '"The Gunners" is the nickname for which football team?' My mind was a blank. Men in the audience, my husband included, were falling off their seats in disbelief that anyone could be so ignorant. Needless to say, the correct answer will lodge in my brain for ever. Arsenal... of course!

Today it seems that quiz shows on television and radio, quiz nights in schools and pubs, as well as a plethora of quiz books, have entered the universal bloodstream to become some of the most popular forms of entertainment. Whatever your age or intellect, there will be a quiz to suit you.

Yet how many of us, having just sat through a quiz programme, would be able to repeat all the correct answers? Most of us would need to hear the programme over and over again before all the information sank in.

So what is our perennial fascination with questions and answers? Does it spring from our earliest quest for information? All small children ask the questions 'Why? When? How? Where? What?' This shows a natural instinctive quest for information, but also a need for the security and comfort that answers can bring. Asking questions is part and parcel of growing up and learning to interact with our environment.

Unlike quiz questions, however, questions about life can rarely be given immediate, concise answers. Often, one question only leads to another and then on to a whole spinning raft of questions that mangle our minds and fray our nerves. Yet it is only by confronting these daily questions that we make our decisions.

When we look at it in that light, it seems extraordinary that our approach to growing in faith is so passive. With busy lives, most people can spare only a fragment of their day to hear or read the Bible, and then it is but a snippet. The parables that Jesus told stand alongside the greatest stories ever told—we love them. The accounts of his miracles have triggered, for many, a longing for similar demonstrations of God's power today, yet they still mystify us. Historians and authors offer books on the subject of Jesus' life—endlessly fascinating to believers and non-believers—but what about the questions that Jesus asked?

In this book, you are invited to explore 20 of those questions. We will delve into the context in which Jesus asked the questions and consider why the people answered him as they did. Then we will take a new approach and try to engage with the questions as if Jesus was putting them directly to us, his present-day disciples. Suddenly, they are not 2000-year-old questions asked of people remote in time and place from us. The stories of those first disciples were written to encourage all who would be disciples in the future, of every age, in every century and continent. Now it is for us, in our time and situation, to work out where we stand in relationship to this same Jesus Christ.

It is not a case of having the 'right' answers. There are no instant, easy or trite replies to the Son of God. But my prayer for you is that you will be open to surprise and challenge as you take time to unravel your own personal answers.

Each chapter contains suggestions to help you wait upon God. In so doing, may you recognize afresh the reality of the living presence of Jesus; may he touch your heart and deepen your faith.

Chapter 1

'What do you want?'

The next day John was there again with two of his disciples. When he saw Jesus passing by, he said, 'Look, the Lamb of God!' When the two disciples heard him say this, they followed Jesus. Turning around, Jesus saw them following and asked, 'What do you want?' They said, 'Rabbi' (which means Teacher), 'where are you staying?' 'Come,' he replied, 'and you will see.' So they went and saw where he was staying, and spent that day with him. It was about the tenth hour. Andrew, Simon Peter's brother, was one of the two who heard what John had said and who had followed Jesus. The first thing Andrew did was to find his brother Simon and tell him, 'We have found the Messiah.'

JOHN 1:35–41

John the Baptist was the last in the Jewish tradition of 'great prophets'. From Mark's Gospel we know that his message of repentance and justice had made an astonishing impact on the people, for we read, 'The whole Judean countryside and all the people of Jerusalem went out to him' (Mark 1:5). That's quite a following. Also, Luke 1:36 gives us the intimate family detail that John the Baptist was a relative of Jesus.

Like all great religious teachers of his day, John had celebrity status and many disciples. His father, Zechariah, being a priest, it would have been natural for young John to grow up immersed in the holy scriptures. Zechariah himself had prophesied for his son, 'And you, my child, will be called a prophet of the Most High; for you will go on before the Lord to prepare the way for him' (Luke 1:76). The background is very important for us to remember as we look at this significant moment recorded by the Gospel writer, the disciple John.

John the Baptist's ministry had reached its climax, the point when he acknowledged that his work was coming to an end. He told his disciples, '[Jesus] must become greater; I must become less' (John 3:30). This was the mark of a truly great man, and Jesus praised him, saying that none had been born greater than John (Matthew 11:11). In these brief verses at the start of John's Gospel, we picture that eccentric, wild-looking prophet staring down the road as his kinsman approaches—but instead of a family greeting, John announces to the two men beside him that Jesus is 'the Lamb of God'.

This strange phrase is rooted way back in Old Testament thought. Remember how the 'Passover lamb' (Exodus 12:21), a male without blemish (v. 5, NRSV), was used to spare God's people from the tenth plague, the death of the firstborn son. The emphasis on Jesus as the 'Lamb of God' was later taken up by Paul in 1 Corinthians 5:7 and by Peter in his first letter (1:19). The phrase is also bound up with the idea of the scapegoat, the animal chased out into the desert bearing the people's sin (Leviticus 16:20–22). John and his disciples would have also known that the image of the lamb was to be found in Isaiah's song of the 'suffering servant' who was 'led like a lamb to the slaughter' (Isaiah 53:7).

Already we can begin to feel the force behind John the Baptist's words. He was stating, in terms understood far better by his hearers than by us today, that Jesus was God's chosen servant, God's anointed, the Messiah. If that wasn't earth-shattering enough, the inference behind his earlier statement that Jesus 'takes away the sin of the world' (John 1:29) was mindblowing. Only God could take away sin!

No wonder the two disciples left their teacher and walked reverently after Jesus. Can you picture the scene? Two men, probably young, are walking a few yards behind the stranger when suddenly he turns round, looks straight at them and asks, 'What do you want?' Like people today who come unexpectedly face to face with somebody famous, they just couldn't think what to say. Unnerved and embarrassed, they came out with a lame reply which had nothing to do with the real reason they wanted to be near Jesus.

We know that one of the men was Andrew. I wonder, who was the other disciple? Could it have been John, who wrote the Gospel? This may have been the first of several encounters with Jesus of Nazareth before John the Baptist was imprisoned and Jesus called them to be his own disciples (Mark 1:14–20).

What were they really wanting? Devout Jews had been longing for centuries for the coming of God's promised Messiah. For Andrew and the others, living under the Roman occupation was humiliating and soul-destroying. It was a political situation that injected a feverish intensity into their longing for both physical and spiritual renewal. Above all, they wanted a Redeemer, a Saviour who would turn all their longings for freedom, justice, forgiveness and peace into triumphant reality. But all they could mutter was, 'Where are you staying?'

What I love about this scene is the way Jesus responded. He invited the men to tag along, no strings attached. There was no condemnation for their halting answer, only a gentle invitation and the opportunity to listen and watch. Notice that verse 39 is quite specific: they only 'spent that day with him'. That taster session was the seed for all that was to follow. They spent a day with the man who would change their lives and the world for ever.

Imagine this same Jesus asking you, 'What do you want?'

Find a quiet place where you won't be disturbed. Indulge yourself with a scented candle. Spend some minutes imagining yourself alongside the two disciples.

Jesus turns to look directly at you. You can see his face, hear his words... He is asking you... 'What do you want?' Allow his words to linger in your mind, to penetrate your heart. Take time to think, time to be honest.

What are your immediate needs? What are you looking for in life? Are you wanting things for those you love? What do *you* want?

If there are many thoughts buzzing in your mind, you might find it helpful to brainstorm a list of what you want—now, at this moment. Write things down in any order, just as they come; the list can always be rearranged later to reflect your priorities. Look at the list long and hard and gradually trace what it is that links all those 'wants' together.

Whatever is bothering you or whatever you are searching for, Jesus understands and is waiting for you to come to him. There may be 'wants' in your list that will not be granted or satisfied in this life but, whatever is uppermost in your heart, Jesus knows. Augustine is quoted as saying, 'We could not have even begun to seek God unless he already had found us.'

Evidently, the ancient rabbis had a standard response to those who came to them with questions. They would say, 'Come and see, and we will think about it together.' What an encouraging reply!

I believe that, just like Andrew and his friend, we need to spend time with Jesus. Maybe there is someone in your life who has pointed you in the right direction, just as John the Baptist pointed his disciples to Jesus. We don't have to be erudite and explain ourselves; we only need to pause, watch and listen.

James Montgomery (1771–1854), one of the vociferous opponents of slavery and the use of child chimney sweeps, has been called the greatest of English lay hymn writers. Here is a verse from one of over 400 hymns that he wrote.

Prayer is the burden of a sigh,
The falling of a tear,
The upward glancing of an eye
When none but God is near.

It doesn't matter if we are diffident, or even if there are times when we don't actually know what we really want. What is important, vitally important if our faith is to strengthen and sustain us, is that we take a step in the right direction—closer to Jesus. The closer we draw to Jesus, the deeper the impact that his teaching will have upon our hearts.

As the apostle James, thought to be Jesus' brother, was to write to the first Jewish Christians living through the dangers and difficulties of sporadic persecution, 'Come near to God and he will come near to you' (James 4:8).

As you open yourself in prayer to God, through Jesus Christ, the answers to your wants, your real wants, will take shape and by the guidance of the Holy Spirit your faith will deepen.

Prayer

Lord Jesus, I bring to you my deepest needs, even the things I cannot share with anyone else. I want to know you as my Saviour. Hold me in your love and surround me with your spirit of peace. Amen

Chapter 2

'Have you never read...?'

One Sabbath Jesus was going through the cornfields, and his disciples began to pick some ears of corn, rub them in their hands and eat the grain. Some of the Pharisees asked, 'Why are you doing what is unlawful on the Sabbath?' Jesus answered them, 'Have you never read what David did when he and his companions were hungry? He entered the house of God, and taking the consecrated bread, he ate what is lawful only for the priests to eat. And he also gave some to his companions.' Then Jesus said to them, 'The Son of Man is Lord of the Sabbath.' On another Sabbath Jesus went into the synagogue and was teaching, and a man was there whose right hand was shrivelled. The Pharisees and the teachers of the law were looking for a reason to accuse Jesus, so they watched him closely to see if he would heal on the Sabbath... Then Jesus said to them, 'I ask you, which is lawful on the Sabbath: to do good or to do evil, to save life or to destroy it?'
LUKE 6:1–7, 9

To spend time browsing in a bookshop is one of my particular pleasures, and should the bookshop have a 'bargain shelf', then I am doubly happy. Usually my purchases are modest and come under the headings of coastal walks, anything to do with China, or vegetarian cooking, but one day I was tempted by a hefty, vivid yellow hardback entitled *Everything You Need to Know in an Emergency*. Well, of course, my life would have been incomplete without this encyclopedia of advice brightening up my study! The book weighed a ton but promised to hold the answer to every cause of distress from burst waterpipe to heart attack. With that tome in my possession, all would be well.

When I came to move house some years later, I had to admit that I had never opened my encyclopedia. I felt a bit ashamed about this until it occurred to me that, in a true emergency, there is no time to go and read a book. Nor do we go about our lives in a state of high expectation and readiness for any and every eventuality. In emergencies we switch to automatic mode and, if possible, call for help. The bulky yellow book went to a charity shop.

My flippant attitude to my ultimately discarded book could not be further removed from the outlook of some of the Pharisees encountered by Jesus. Their whole life's work was about imposing ritual laws on every conceivable aspect of daily living. Their motivation could be construed as honourably devout or a way of distancing themselves and their culture from the despised Roman occupiers. At all costs they worked to retain Judaism's purity: they saw it as their duty to preserve their national identity because, for them, national and religious identity were the same.

No doubt the Pharisees prided themselves on representing a fundamental movement of renewal, as opposed to the Sadducees, who were content to compromise with Rome in order to secure their position and influence. We only have to look at the various political and religious groups today, with their factions and bickering, to be reminded that similar power struggles formed the backdrop to Jesus' ministry.

When we read the verses from Luke's Gospel at the beginning of this chapter, we should forget the vast hectares that modern agriculture calls 'fields'. Jesus and his disciples were wandering along the pathways beside strips of land (like those cultivated by villagers under our medieval feudal system), planted with corn. Obviously, they were not alone. Imagine Jesus, the twelve disciples, women and children, curious villagers, critical Pharisees—possibly as many as 30 or 40 people trekking from one Galilean village to another.

Technically, the disciples were not doing anything wrong by pulling off some corn and creating some makeshift muesli. They could not be accused of stealing, as the Law of Moses said, 'If you enter your neighbour's cornfield, you may pick the ears with your hands, but you must not put a sickle to the standing corn' (Deuteronomy 23:25), but the Pharisees immediately jumped on the fact that the disciples were breaking the sabbath laws by 'working'. The Jewish legal tradition had built up an incredible 39 categories of activity forbidden on the sabbath, including 'reaping'. These traditions were creatively embellished so that any form of work became anathema on the sabbath, and, in the blinkered eyes of the Pharisees, healing was aligned with 'work'.

It is tempting to scoff at this religious absurdity, but obviously Mark, Matthew and Luke decided that it was necessary to record it as an expression of the different emphases in the teaching of Jesus and the Pharisees.

Jesus turned the criticism back on the Pharisees themselves. They were meticulous and learned men: they had read how their national icon, King David, some thousand years before, had eaten bread designated for priests alone. In the account (see 1 Samuel 21:1–6), David put the well-being of himself and his soldiers above strict manmade rules. His action did not become a habit; it was his response to an emergency. (Sadly, I'll never know whether advice for a similar emergency was given in my yellow book!) David needed food, which became available just at the right time. To him, it was yet another illustration of God's provision for his people.

It was bad enough for the Pharisees to be reminded of King David's actions, but Jesus went on to silence them with a sensational claim about himself: 'The Son of Man is Lord of the Sabbath' (Luke 6:5). Again, Mark, Matthew and Luke all record Jesus using the phrase 'Son of Man' about himself. The well-read Pharisees would have recognized it as a term used for Daniel, the great prophet of the exile. So Jesus left them in no doubt that his authority was beyond theirs. They could not control him and, by healing the man with the shrivelled hand, he exposed their self-righteous pride for the sham it had become. The Pharisees' obsession with rules made them content to withhold, on the sabbath, food from the hungry and healing from the sick. By his actions, Jesus taught that God does not expect us to neglect our neighbours in pursuit of holiness. Rather, we honour and glorify God by 'doing good' (v. 9).

Although we may interpret his ministry as challenging the narrow-minded legalism rife among the religious leaders of his time, Jesus made sure his followers knew exactly where he stood: 'Do not think that I have come to abolish the Law or the Prophets; I have not come to abolish them but to fulfil them' (Matthew 5:17). Jesus revealed a God of mercy and justice, whose love was inclusive and eternal, a God whom he called 'Abba', Father. To the eager crowds whose spiritual appetite had been whetted by the preaching of John the Baptist, this was true liberation theology.

Before we begin to feel complacent, perhaps we need to take a look at ourselves.

Many people are put off Christianity because they think it is a religion of rules: a catalogue of 'Thou shalt nots'. Sadly, those who feel like this have not taken time to read the summary of the laws, the Ten Commandments, together with the teaching of Jesus, the fulfilment of God's law. The Victorian clergyman and hymn writer Frederick William Faber (1814–63) wrote some piercing lines:

> But we make his love too narrow
> By false limits of our own;
> And we magnify his strictness
> With a zeal he will not own.

> If our love were but more simple
> We should take him at his word;
> And our lives would be illumined
> By the presence of our Lord.

The Pharisees made life so complicated. It was as if the more they tied themselves in knots of religious practice, the more those same knots strangled their capacity for the values Jesus taught. Their hearts were not fertile ground for the fruit of the Spirit, which Paul listed as 'love, joy, peace, patience, kindness, goodness, faithfulness, gentleness and self-control' (Galatians 5:22–23). The listening crowds were witnessing an ever widening gap between Jesus and their religious leaders as Jesus gave the words of scripture fresh life and purpose. He taught that there is no room in God's kingdom for spite and envy, criticism, rigid tunnel vision and cold self-righteousness. He brought them the healing joys of forgiveness, of sharing and mutual concern. If they could manage to live the way he taught, they would truly live as God intended humankind to live in the original paradise of Eden.

Let's take this account of Jesus' healing and teaching at the most basic level.

- Jesus is not only Lord of the sabbath but also Lord of our lives.
- Jesus shows us that there is no virtue in putting rules before human need.
- Jesus gave his disciples a proactive message—to do good.

The scenario is reminiscent of Moses' words in Deuteronomy 30:19: 'I have set before you life and death, blessings and curses. Now choose life.' Jesus posed the choice between good and evil, to save life or to destroy it. In case you don't have your Bible handy to check what reply the Pharisees gave, I can tell you that none is recorded!

As we look back over missed opportunities in our lives, the occasions when we have said and done things we never intended and bitterly regret, the times of doubt or downright disbelief, can we hear Jesus whispering to us, 'Have you never read…'?

The Pharisees had plenty of head knowledge of God's forgiveness and love but, because of their closed minds, they restricted God's word for their own convenience. They chose to ignore any teaching that interfered with their routine.

Sometimes we too may fall into the temptation to pick and

choose the stories and parables we like while disregarding the challenging parts. Our minds and hearts can also remain closed, either by ignorance or by choice, leaving us with a sadly restricted and erroneous impression of our Saviour and his message.

A traditional story tells of a fly living in a world-famous art gallery. One day the fly alighted on a section of canvas that was dull to his eyes and rough to his tiny feet. The fly decided he didn't like this painting and he would never land on it again. If only he had seen the whole picture, though, he would have realized that it wasn't all dull and rough. He would have seen that he had made his judgment on the merest centimetre of paint brushed there by the great artist Van Gogh. The fly never saw the vibrant sunflowers.

As Paul wrote to his young friend Timothy, 'All scripture is God-breathed and is useful for teaching, rebuking, correcting and training in righteousness' (2 Timothy 3:16).

Prayer

Lord, guide me by your Holy Spirit so that I may see your purpose for me on the canvas of my life. Give me a desire to read more and more of your word as I seek to grow in your love and grace.

Chapter 3

'And why do you worry about clothes?'

'Therefore I tell you, do not worry about your life, what you will eat or drink; or about your body, what you will wear. Is not life more important than food, and the body more important than clothes? Look at the birds of the air; they do not sow or reap or store away in barns, and yet your heavenly Father feeds them. Are you not much more valuable than they? Who of you by worrying can add a single hour to his life? And why do you worry about clothes? See how the lilies of the field grow. They do not labour or spin. Yet I tell you that not even Solomon in all his splendour was dressed like one of these. If that is how God clothes the grass of the field, which is here today and tomorrow is thrown into the fire, will he not much more clothe you, O you of little faith? So do not worry, saying, "What shall we eat?" or "What shall we drink?" or "What shall we wear?" For the pagans run after all these things, and your heavenly Father knows that you need them. But seek first his kingdom and his righteousness, and all these things will be given to you as well. Therefore do not worry about tomorrow, for tomorrow will worry about itself. Each day has enough trouble of its own.'
MATTHEW 6:25–34

It sounds as though the disciples had been fussing! These twelve men had taken a momentous step to become disciples of Jesus, relinquishing their jobs and walking away from their homes. Is it any wonder that the enormity of what they had done was causing them anxiety? After all, which of us, after taking a life-changing decision, has not wrestled with those niggling doubts when the first burst of enthusiasm has subsided?

Maybe it had dawned on Peter, James, Matthew and the others that life as an itinerant disciple was not quite as rosy as they had expected and, at times, seemed full of uncertainties and insecurity. Sometimes they were a long way from the nearest village and food supply ('This is a remote place...' Matthew 14:15). What on earth were they going to eat? They were moving around the countryside —their clothes wouldn't last for ever—they would need 'better' garments for going up to Jerusalem, and leather boots for winter... All these valid concerns were evidently sprinkled through their conversations.

Jesus heard their worries and knew that his men, just like us, could win medals in the art of worrying. So when he went up on the mountainside and sat down to deliver the famous teaching that we call the Sermon on the Mount, he incorporated a special word for the worriers.

Over the past two decades, I've visited the Holy Land in several different seasons, and it has been marvellous to sample the variety of weather and scenery with which our Lord would have been familiar. Until very recently, however, I'd never been in Galilee in February. Wild flowers dotted the landscape in multicoloured clumps of yellow mustard, scarlet anemones, white daisies, violet Maltese Cross flowers and wild irises mingled with many other indigenous plants. It made me think that perhaps it was early spring when Jesus gave this teaching. Seated on the hill in warm sunshine overlooking the Sea of Galilee and surrounded by a glorious natural carpet, he used 'the lilies of the field' as the perfect visual aid (vv. 28–29).

I'm no botanical expert but I know enough to recognize the exquisite beauty of petals and scent, the precision of flowering and reproduction, and the potential for each seed to burst into new life. I'm no 'twitcher' but I love to watch the swallows constructing their nest with only a beak and two little feet. Their instinctive ingenuity and skill leave me spellbound. Jesus used those simple sights, which are common the world over, to open his disciples' eyes of faith. If God has created the birds and flowers with such loving care, how much more will he provide and care for us! In the context of life and death, peace and war, hunger and thirst, clothes would come under the heading of 'trivia'. The disciples did not need to be overly concerned about such matters.

Sadly, most of us know people about whom it can be said, 'If they haven't got anything to worry about, they have to find something.' Worry grabs us all at some point in our lives: we worry over health, children, parents, finances, work, weather conditions—the list has no end. We cannot help being concerned for those we love but when worry takes a stranglehold on our lives it destroys our capacity to live in the present moment. Worry can become literally disabling and, when it takes such a hold, then God is pushed away.

The disciples had food and they were clothed, but they were projecting their worries into the future. Too much focus on the future, and what might go wrong in it, can taint our gratitude for the present.

Jesus not only asked, 'Why do you worry…?' He offered a framework of seven ways to counteract worry. Remember the importance in scripture of the number seven, standing for completeness. Jesus outlined the complete antidote to worry, although I suspect that the disciples were as frail as we are when it came to letting go of their concerns. Jesus probably repeated this teaching on many occasions, and Matthew memorized his Lord's words. Our grateful thanks go to him for enabling us, two millennia later, to read the words of Jesus addressing our worries today.

1 Sort out your priorities (v. 25). What is really important to you? When people are recovering from serious illness, they often comment that the experience has given them a new perspective on life. It is all too easy to lose such perspective in the bustle of the everyday world.

2 Look at God's creation (v. 26). Think of yourself as God's beloved creation also, part of his great design. Consider how you were formed in the womb, and remember the people who have been part of your life. How miraculous it is that God loves us so much that even the hairs on our head are numbered! (Matthew 10:30).

3 Remember that worrying does not alter our situation (v. 27). It has no effect on external events, but has a calamitous effect upon our inner reserves of patience, strength and ability to cope. Jesus spared no punches: worrying was, and is, a useless preoccupation. Life is too short to waste time on it.

4 Think of King Solomon (vv. 28–30). With all his vast wealth, he could clothe himself like no one else, but he had nothing to compare with God's colours and designs. How arrogant to think that we can better God, who created us, who loves us with an everlasting love, who will never abandon us!

5 Believe that all of life is in our heavenly Father's hands (vv. 31–32). When I read these verses, I feel that Jesus is saying to me, 'Yes, everybody in the world worries but, if you believe in me, you should know better.' When we enter into a relationship with the living Son of God, life's problems don't suddenly disappear but, as someone once said, we realize that 'faith is putting your hand out in the darkness and finding it held'.

6 Put first things first (v. 33). The prophet Micah wrote, 'What does the Lord require of you? To act justly and to love mercy and to walk humbly with your God' (6:8). Jesus gave the prophet's words his own emphasis: 'Seek first his kingdom...' Instead of worrying in our own strength, we need to concentrate on living by the principles of the kingdom of heaven—justice, mercy, peace. Giving these values prime position in our life, in our attitude and dealings with others, will take a supreme effort if our worries are to take a back seat.

7   Take one day at a time (v. 34). There is no virtue in overload and no advantage in trying to second-guess tomorrow. After all, today is the tomorrow you worried about yesterday! There is an old hymn by Edward Joy that I remember from my childhood: 'All your anxiety, all your care, bring to the mercy-seat, leave it there.'

'Why do you worry?' Let these words penetrate your heart and mind. Imagine that Jesus is asking you, 'Why do you worry?' Why do you? Give him your reasons. Then take Jesus at his word, and meditate on this promise from Psalm 55:22: 'Cast your cares on the Lord and he will sustain you.' Leave those cares and worries with him; don't pick them up again and trudge on heavily through the day.

Prayer

Lord, I bring to you all the cares and concerns that weigh me down. Fill me, I pray, with your peace, the peace that no one else can give.

Chapter 4

'Why are you so afraid?'

That day when evening came, [Jesus] said to his disciples, 'Let us go over to the other side.' Leaving the crowd behind, they took him along, just as he was, in the boat. There were also other boats with him. A furious squall came up, and the waves broke over the boat, so that it was nearly swamped. Jesus was in the stern, sleeping on a cushion. The disciples woke him and said to him, 'Teacher, don't you care if we drown?' He got up, rebuked the wind and said to the waves, 'Quiet! Be still!' Then the wind died down and it was completely calm. He said to his disciples, 'Why are you so afraid? Do you still have no faith?' They were terrified and asked each other, 'Who is this? Even the wind and the waves obey him!'
MARK 4:35–41

Most of my life has been spent in Cornwall, the county with the longest coastline in Britain. In fact, apart from four miles of land in the north of the county, Cornwall is divided from Devon by the River Tamar and is therefore almost an island. On many occasions, local television news has shown dramatic lifeboat rescues in the most appalling sea conditions, which seem a million miles away from the calm, blue waters that we imagine the Sea of Galilee to be. The geological position of that lake, however, 209 metres below sea level and surrounded by towering hills, makes it particularly susceptible to wild storms that blow up without warning.

One of those storms happened back in 1934. So violent did the water become that many homes along the shoreline at Tiberias were swept away and several people were drowned—proof that the Gospel writer Mark was not exaggerating in his account of the fearsome storm described in our Bible passage here. That dark night on Galilee, even the bravest of the fishermen among the disciples—men who had endured storms before and knew every inch of the lake—felt that they were in the grip of disaster. What words might have come to their minds as they baled rising water from the boat and shouted to their master to wake up?

In the great book of Psalms, we find poetry brimming with every emotion, and there are two in particular that give a whole new dimension to this nature miracle. First, if we turn to Psalm 65:5–7, we read, 'O God our Saviour, the hope of all the ends of the earth... who stilled the roaring of the seas...' Then, in Psalm 89:8–9, we find, 'O Lord God Almighty, who is like you? You are mighty, O Lord, and your faithfulness surrounds you. You rule over the surging sea; when its waves mount up, you still them.'

These psalms were written centuries back in Israel's history, and their significance lies in the way the well-known words would have resonated in the minds of Jesus' disciples. The power to still raging seas belonged to the Sovereign God of Israel, the Creator of heaven and earth—and the disciples were witnessing this power in action from their own master.

Jesus, their teacher, the man they ate and laughed with, the friend who stayed with Peter's family and who told such gripping stories... suddenly they were afraid of him. Who was he? Surely he was a man of God, but could he be...?

Sometimes we are so captivated by this dramatic miracle that we overlook seven little words almost hidden within Mark's account: 'There were also other boats with him' (v. 36b). This was not a miracle just for the benefit of the disciples with him in the boat; it was a public demonstration, to all the boats on the sea that night, that they were in the presence of God.

We know that Simon Peter and his brother Andrew, the brothers James and John, and Philip were fishermen. The Gospels tell us that Matthew was a tax collector and Jesus himself was a carpenter. There is no mention of the other disciples' occupations before they joined Jesus so they may well have been non-fishermen. As we imagine some combination of these followers, soaking wet and frightened to death, Jesus' question 'Why are you so afraid?' appears somewhat harsh. After all, in those circumstances, who wouldn't be afraid?

Let's try to look at the question from Jesus' point of view, though. The disciples had previously witnessed his power and authority; they had seen miracles. Why, then, when Jesus was with them, should these tough men dissolve in terror? Didn't they trust him?

The simple and honest answer is 'No'. They were overawed by their physical surroundings and by their own inadequacy. They reacted in the same way as they would have done before Jesus had come into their lives. I warm to these men—they were real. They panicked just as I panic. Don't we all panic at times when we rely on our own understanding and strength rather than putting our trust in God? So how would we answer Jesus if he sat alongside us and asked, 'Why are *you* so afraid?'

When I was growing up, the common fear was the threat of the 'Cold War' and the ramifications of nuclear warfare, but now the Cold War has melted into history and terrorist attacks and flu pandemics are more immediate and personal fears. We could also list a host of phobias—fear of heights, spiders, snakes, open spaces and so on—that terrify and socially paralyse hundreds of thousands of people. Perhaps the greatest fear in today's Western world is the fear of death. All such fears are in stark contrast to what Jesus offers his followers: 'I have come that they may have life, and have it to the full' (John 10:10). He also said to his disciples, 'Peace I leave with you; my peace I give you... Do not let your hearts be troubled and do not be afraid' (14:27), a passage that is often used at funeral services. We can take heart also from the words of the elderly John, writing to a church shadowed by intense persecution: 'There is no fear in love. But perfect love drives out fear' (1 John 4:18).

Richard was just four years old when his parents took a caravan holiday in the Wye Valley on the border between England and

Wales. It was the little boy's first experience away from his home in the middle of Bristol and he was as excited as a four-year-old could be. But in the night he woke his parents, sobbing and shaking. He was frightened by a strange noise outside the caravan. Realizing what it was, his father wrapped the boy up, took him in his arms and went outside into the darkness. When they heard the noise again, and his father explained that it was only a beautiful bird, an owl hooting, Richard stopped shaking. He was safe in his father's arms.

The testimony of the Gospel makes it plain that Almighty God, through Jesus Christ, brought calm to the turbulent waters of Galilee. He 'saved' the boat. The testimony of Christians down the centuries and in our own time encourages us to put our trembling trust in him. We need to take our own step in faith, to believe that this same God, in and through his Son, will give us peace to work through the storms that threaten to overwhelm us. He will save us.

For reflection

In a quiet place, jot down your fears or, if they are too painful to acknowledge on paper, hold your Bible and tell Jesus how you feel. When you have had time with your own thoughts and prayers, you might like to read the following meditation (perhaps out loud, to make it more personal).

These words were written by a friend of mine who was on pilgrimage to the Holy Land and went out in a wooden boat on the Sea of Galilee. As you read, feel yourself held in your heavenly Father's arms.

Jesus sits in the boat peacefully sleeping. The calm waters are surrounded by the magnificent hills of the Golan Heights, Mount Arbel and the lower hills of Galilee.

There is a gentle breeze, followed by a strong wind. The boat rocks to and fro, gently at first, then the ripples turn into waves. The boat moves from side to side, up and down. The water no longer laps against the boat. It splashes, becoming louder and stronger.

As the boat rocks, it begins to take on water. The gentle breeze is now a howling wind. I hear the wind whistling, almost screaming past my ears, but Jesus is still asleep. How can this be? Is he unaware of the dangers facing me?

I wake him from his slumber, for I am afraid—afraid the boat will capsize and I will drown. What does Jesus do? Of all the questions he could have asked, he says, 'Why are you afraid?'

Afraid? I am petrified! Can he not see? Does he not care? I may drown and he asks, 'Why are you afraid?' Surely he can see my situation.

But Jesus, being the calm person he is, stands up, puts forth his hands and firmly says, 'Be still.'

Be still? He must be joking! But… no. 'Be still!' The wind subsides, the waves die down and the water becomes calm.

I am amazed—I don't know why. Did I not know that Jesus would not forsake me at this time? Where has my faith gone? 'O you of little faith' —that was me.

Through all my trials and tribulations, he is there. When the waters get rough, he is there. He is my strength; I must trust him. I must have faith and he will bring me through the winds and rough seas into the calm of his everlasting love, grace and peace.

XANDY MOULD

'How many loaves do you have?'

The apostles gathered around Jesus and reported to him all they had done and taught. Then, because so many people were coming and going that they did not even have a chance to eat, he said to them, 'Come with me by yourselves to a quiet place and get some rest.' So they went away by themselves in a boat to a solitary place. But many who saw them leaving recognized them and ran on foot from all the towns and got there ahead of them. When Jesus landed and saw a large crowd, he had compassion on them, because they were like sheep without a shepherd. So he began teaching them many things. By this time it was late in the day, so his disciples came to him. 'This is a remote place,' they said, 'and it's already very late. Send the people away so that they can go to the surrounding countryside and villages and buy themselves something to eat.' But Jesus answered, 'You give them something to eat.' They said to him, 'That would take eight months of a man's wages! Are we to go and spend that much on bread and give it to them to eat?' 'How many loaves do you have?' he asked. 'Go and see.'

MARK 6:30–38

Such was the impact of what we call 'the feeding of the five thousand' that all four Gospel authors felt it was vital to include it (see Matthew 14:13–21; Luke 9:10–17; John 6:1–15). In fact, it is the only miracle described by all four writers. Let's try to bed ourselves deep into this, perhaps one of the best-known of all Jesus' miracles.

First of all, the backstory. Mark tells us that Jesus had been home to Nazareth, the town where he grew up with his family. We can probably assume that Joseph was dead by this time as people were referring to Jesus as 'the carpenter... Mary's son' (6:3). Mark also mentions Jesus' younger brothers, James (who was to become the first leader of the church in Jerusalem: see Acts 15:13), Joseph, Judas and Simon. Typically, the girls are not mentioned by name but merely recorded as 'his sisters'! The home visit had been less than successful, however, and Jesus and his followers had taken themselves out of Nazareth, journeying down the valley roads towards Capernaum on the shore of the Sea of Galilee. Almost certainly, they would have stopped with friends in Cana (John 2:2).

Somewhere along the way between Nazareth and the lakeside villages by Galilee, Jesus commissioned his twelve disciples for their first 'mission' experience (Mark 6:6–13). They were to take his message into the communities in the area, teaching and healing in their master's name.

They fanned out in pairs among the villages, reiterating the words Jesus had taught them, just as disciples of the prophets and rabbis had done centuries before. The sick were anointed with oil and many were healed. Only on this one occasion does Mark call them 'apostles' (v. 30), meaning 'messengers' or 'envoys' of Jesus, and they returned excited and full of their first experience of mission, bursting to share with Jesus all the details of what they had been doing in his name.

Imagine, then, what a shadow must have been cast over their endeavours when news reached them that John the Baptist had been brutally murdered (vv. 14–29).

John was not just another prophet: he was family. Jesus' mother, Mary, and Elizabeth, John's mother, were cousins. Shock, anger, anguish and fear would have gripped the whole group. No wonder Jesus suggested they go 'away to a deserted place' (v. 31b, NRSV) to rest. The last thing they wanted to see was a swarm of people pressing to hear Jesus after their arrival in the supposedly 'deserted' place. I feel sure that James and John, the 'sons of thunder' (3:17), would have done some pretty uncharitable muttering into their beards!

Jesus, however, tired and grieving as he was, still had compassion for the people. As he looked at the crowd, milling around waiting for words of hope and comfort, Jesus felt their vulnerability. They seemed lost and leaderless, like sheep without a shepherd, and so he began 'teaching them many things' (v. 34). Mark does not record exactly what Jesus taught on this occasion, but we may assume it included the good news that although they were a desolate and occupied people, they were known and loved by God. Jesus was so much more than a travelling healer. Every miraculous healing was performed to the glory of God and so that people might be spiritually reborn. Every parable held a message to underline God's forgiveness and unconditional love.

In the end, the disciples came and interrupted the impromptu teaching session. Underlying their remark that it was 'very late' (v. 35), we can hear the disciples saying, 'Look, Master, tell all these people to go away. We've had enough for one day.' They weren't expecting the reply that Jesus gave them. All they wanted was to get shot of these trespassers on their time, have something to eat and get a break from the crowds.

Jesus had other ideas. He knew how his disciples felt but, in the question he asked, he offered them (and us) a lesson in true compassion: 'How many loaves do you have?'

Was this the cue for more grumblings into beards? Jesus knew they were tired; why should he give them any more to do? We, too, fall into the temptation of feeling that we've done our bit and it's time for somebody else to take over, but the compassion of Jesus sets a standard above our natural inclinations. If we are to be his followers, our focus needs to be not on what we have done or think we deserve, but on what others need. Chivvied by Jesus, his irritable disciples were changed into instruments of blessing—the miracle of the multiplication became iconic, a symbol of God's endless provision—and those twelve weary, grudging men were part of a momentous event.

Without their obedience, we would never have received this wonderful story. It's a miracle that gives us a compelling illustration of conversion—from hunger to plenty, from individual possession to the fellowship of corporate sharing, from disbelief to faith.

As news of this feeding miracle permeated the surrounding towns and villages and spread ever wider, with more and more people talking about Jesus of Nazareth, there would have been one resounding echo in Jewish ears: 'He humbled you, causing you to hunger and then feeding you with manna' (Deuteronomy 8:3). They would have remembered the exodus, when the Hebrew slaves were brought out of Egypt by Moses, wandered in the desert and were miraculously fed by God. Deep in Jewish hearts was a belief in the providential care of their God, as well as their almost sacramental attitude to sharing food together.

So what does Jesus' question mean for us: 'How many loaves do you have?'

I recall the words of Revd Jeffrey Sharp, a minister who had a great influence on my journey of faith while I myself was training for the ministry: 'Never say you don't have enough time, and never say you do not have enough resources.' I have to admit, there have been many times when I have wailed for the lack of both time and resources, but on each occasion those words have come to mind. God does not ask us to do the impossible, to be omnipotent champions in the Christian life, but in the question 'How many loaves do you have?' we are prompted to lift our eyes beyond our own strength. Self-sufficiency is a lonely virtue. When we offer our time and resources to God, just as Jesus gave thanks over the loaves and fish, we glimpse the power of compassion and the blessing that comes through sharing.

As I write this chapter, it is December, and charity catalogues are offering some unusual Christmas presents this year. Fruit trees, school textbooks, sanitation blocks, immunization packs, as well as chickens and goats—all are available for donors to 'buy' and thus ensure that they are sent to help communities in developing countries.

One of my friends got thoroughly involved with one of these projects and broadcast among her office colleagues what she and her church were doing. The result was another miracle of multiplication. With her colleagues—people from all different faiths and none—she raised nearly £1000, which enabled their chosen charity to purchase several of the larger items to make life safer and healthier for others. Those 'others' are our brothers and sisters in God's family.

Julia Perkes wasn't famous; she led an ordinary, comfortable family life and had a fulfilling job nursing in a Dorset hospital. Often, in her work, Julia nursed terminally ill children and it was a cruel blow when she discovered that she herself was suffering from cancer. During her illness, however, Julia held a passionate desire: she dreamed of a hospice to cater for children in her own locality who were suffering from life-threatening illnesses. Others caught the dream and her project began to turn from vision to a realistic possibility. Sadly, Julia didn't live to see the building and final opening of the hospice that was to bear her name—Julia's House. Nevertheless, she had the satisfaction of knowing that other people were drawn together to work for this aim. In the end, many more than five thousand people got involved, and are still working together.

One person *can* make a difference. All it takes is obedience to the teaching of our Lord, hearing his question to us, and looking into our lives to discover what resources we have been given. Then, in the power of the Holy Spirit, we can offer what we have in God's service.

How many 'loaves' do we have? Perhaps we've never stopped to find out what resources God has already provided for us. There are so many ways in which we can show compassion and address the needs of others. We only need to follow Jesus' prompting: 'Go and see.'

Prayer

Lord, I pray today for all those who serve others—professionally, voluntarily or as carers in the home. Help me to discern my own opportunities to make a difference in and through the name of Jesus Christ my Lord. Amen

Chapter 6

'Will you give me a drink?'

Now (Jesus) had to go through Samaria. So he came to a town in Samaria called Sychar, near the plot of ground Jacob had given to his son Joseph. Jacob's well was there, and Jesus, tired as he was from the journey, sat down by the well. It was about the sixth hour. When a Samaritan woman came to draw water, Jesus said to her, 'Will you give me a drink?' (His disciples had gone into the town to buy food.) The Samaritan woman said to him, 'You are a Jew and I am a Samaritan woman. How can you ask me for a drink?' (For Jews do not associate with Samaritans.) Jesus answered her, 'If you knew the gift of God and who it is that asks you for a drink, you would have asked him and he would have given you living water.' 'Sir,' the woman said, 'you have nothing to draw with and the well is deep. Where can you get this living water? Are you greater than our father Jacob...?' Jesus answered, 'Everyone who drinks this water will be thirsty again, but whoever drinks the water I give him will never thirst. Indeed, the water I give him will become in him a spring of water welling up to eternal life.'
JOHN 4:4–14

Several years ago, the film crew for the long-running children's television programme *Blue Peter* were on location in one of the African countries. With the cameras rolling, they came across the body of a small boy, crumpled and left by the roadside. It was heart-wrenching to see the little scrap, deserted in such barren surroundings. Suddenly one of the crew thought they saw a tremor in the wasted flesh. They raced over and put some water to the boy's lips. Millions of children, watching the programme later, witnessed a miracle as life came back into the child. It not only made an inspiring 'good news' item; it perfectly illustrated how essential water is to life.

The Bible, with its stories of people living in a hot, dry climate, gives water a significance that is lost to our tap-turning, water-wasting nation. It is so much easier to grasp the spiritual parallels in this passage from John 4 when you live in a country where water is precious. Before we consider the importance of water, though, we need to paint the scenery against which this drama is set.

What an intriguing sentence John wrote: 'Now he had to go through Samaria' (v. 4) Why? Yes, it was the shortest route between Jerusalem and Galilee—it was used as a commercial highway—but Jesus could have taken the longer, less controversial route along the Jordan valley. What was the urgency?

This is so much more than a story of 'conversion by the well'. The immediate audience would have been outraged and perplexed by Jesus' behaviour but, as we shall see, those who chose to take on board Jesus' teaching found the key to ethnic coexistence and gender equality.

The animosity between Jews and Samaritans had a sorry history. After the peaceful reign of King Solomon, the land became divided into a northern and a southern kingdom, with Sychar (or Shechem) and Jerusalem as the capital cities of north and south respectively. The northern kingdom of Samaria was besieged by the Assyrians for three years, until 721BC, when it was captured and much of the population deported to Assyria (2 Kings 17:6). The Assyrians then imported people from other areas to live in Samaria. These people, over the years, intermarried with the remaining Jews of the northern kingdom, which meant that the Jews forfeited their racial purity.

Some two hundred years after the fall of the northern kingdom, the southern kingdom fell to the Babylonians, who took the vast majority of Jews into exile in Babylon in 586BC (2 Kings 24:8–17). These Jews, in exile, retained their racial purity. When they eventually returned to Judea and began to rebuild their sacred temple in Jerusalem, the Samaritans offered to help them but received a stern rebuff: 'You have no part with us in building a temple to our God' (Ezra 4:1–3). Worse was to come. Having been excluded from building the temple in Jerusalem, the Samaritans built their own rival temple on Mount Gerazim.

Sadly, in 138BC, during the time of the Maccabees, a Jew called John Hyrcanus destroyed the Mount Gerazim temple. By the time of Jesus, a deep and bitter hatred had existed between the Jews and Samaritans for more than 400 years. Rabbis even forbade Jews to eat from Samaritan utensils. Some extremist Samaritans would light straw and drop a smouldering bundle behind any Jew walking through their town in order to burn away their footprints from the land.

So now we have this curious picture of Jesus sitting by Jacob's well in the heat of the day while his disciples are shopping in a nearby Samaritan market. This particular area was steeped in historical significance for both Jew and Samaritan with its links to two great icons from the past, Jacob and Joseph. It was an important site for groundbreaking teaching.

The second shock in this story comes when Jesus actually speaks to the Samaritan woman. She herself is taken aback, as verse 9 makes clear. Strict rabbis were forbidden to speak to any woman in public, so the fact that Jesus, a Jew, spoke to this Samaritan woman was all the more astounding.

Yet Jesus broke through all these barriers. His teaching, by word and action, demonstrated the inclusive love of God. It was a teaching so radical that, like Jacob's dream in that same vicinity (Genesis 28:12), it became a bridge between heaven and earth, God and his people, Jew and Samaritan.

We hardly ever think of Jesus as he is described in this story—hot, tired and thirsty. The 'sixth hour' (v. 6) was 12 noon, the hottest time of day, when no sensible person would go to collect water at the well. This has fuelled speculation that the Samaritan woman's lifestyle made her socially unacceptable in her own community. In verses 17 and 18 we find out that she has had five husbands (unusual, to say the least); neither is she married to the current man in her life. She comes to the well to avoid the looks and comments… only to be approached by another man!

Most men of that time, if they had spoken at all, would have ordered the woman to give them a drink, but Jesus makes a request, not a command. She could have turned away but instead she finds herself in conversation with the enigmatic stranger.

Then, following on from his physical need for water, Jesus begins to engage the woman in a theology that she would have instantly recognized. The prophet Jeremiah had written of 'the Lord, the spring of living water' (Jeremiah 17:13). Isaiah, writing about the day of the Lord, or the reign of the Messiah, wrote, 'With joy you will draw water from the wells of salvation' (Isaiah 12:3). In using the phrase 'living water', Jesus was unmistakably declaring himself not only greater than the patriarch Jacob, but on a par with God— blatantly making a messianic claim.

Like the Jews, the Samaritans were also waiting for 'the promised one'. Their hope of a Messiah was based on Deuteronomy 18:15–18, which describes the coming of a prophet, one who would tell them everything God commanded.

In these few verses in John's Gospel we see how Jesus is transformed in the eyes of the woman from a stranger into 'the Christ', while she herself is transformed from a social outcast into an excited witness of the gospel. Such is the power of encounter with the living water.

I've been thinking long and hard about how I would react to Jesus' question, 'Will you give me a drink?' My first thought is, 'I have nothing good enough to offer the Lord of life.' In the previous chapter, we were thinking about how God takes and multiplies our resources for his glory, so perhaps we should focus once more on God's provision rather than our limitations.

In the feeding of the five thousand, the disciples had limited resources to offer but God opened their eyes to see that miracles can happen when we give him those resources. Only God, though Jesus, can truly enable the transformation of our finite drops of water. Transformed through the gift of his Holy Spirit, mere drops become the living, gushing waters, overwhelming us with the blessing of eternal life.

We can also make a link with Jesus' words in Matthew 25: 'I was thirsty and you gave me something to drink... whatever you did for one of the least of these brothers and sisters of mine, you did for me' (vv. 35, 40).

Thinking globally, we have 'brothers and sisters' in the human family across the planet. Heart-rending statistics such as the fact that a child dies every 15 seconds from infected water grab our attention—and we can do something about it. As church groups or as individuals, we can play our part in helping others have their rightful access to clean water, and in doing so, we are doing it for Jesus himself.

This is where it gets uncomfortable. Could this be the way we might answer Jesus' question? By the transformation of our attitudes, our horizons, our prejudices and our priorities? It was John Wesley, some 250 years ago, who declared to 18th-century England, 'There is no holiness without social holiness.' When in Bristol and London, he had made appeals for clean straw and food for French prisoners of war and the sick and destitute, and from the money he earned from his writings he supported many members of his family.

The task is so enormous that it is easy to be swallowed up by despair, but let's hear Jesus ask us that question again. Let it seep into our hearts: 'Will you give me a drink?'

These words are spoken to *you*. Pause and ponder them. What will you do?

Prayer

Lord, forgive me when I feel defeated by other people's desperate needs. Give me courage when I'm tempted to give up. Help me to be your hands and feet at the meeting places in my own community, your voice for the voiceless and your love for those who are hurting. In your name, may I cross barriers and build bridges of hope. Amen

Chapter 7

'Do you want to leave too?'

Many of his disciples said, 'This is a hard teaching. Who can accept it?' Aware that his disciples were grumbling about this, Jesus said to them, 'Does this offend you? What if you see the Son of Man ascend to where he was before! The Spirit gives life; the flesh counts for nothing. The words I have spoken to you are spirit and they are life. Yet there are some of you who do not believe.' For Jesus had known from the beginning which of them did not believe and who would betray him. He went on to say, 'This is why I told you that no one can come to me unless the Father has enabled them.' From this time many of his disciples turned back and no longer followed him. 'You do not want to leave too, do you?' Jesus asked the Twelve.
JOHN 6:60–67

When a famous football team is winning trophies and at the top of the game, the stadium crowds are enormous. Sales of shirts, mugs, scarves and photographs reach record levels and everyone, from the board of directors and the manager to the coach and members of the fan club, is happy.

If the great team then loses a couple of games, starts slipping down the league table, and fuels a few unpleasant newspaper articles with some reckless scandal, it is frightening how quickly the mood of supporters can turn hostile. The people grumble and numbers in the stands slump, sales of club merchandise take a nosedive and the manager usually gets the sack. The general public can be chillingly fickle; only true fans stick with their team through thick and thin, through good seasons and bad.

The number of people drawn to Jesus by his awesome miracles

grew by the day. Sometimes the crowds were so intrusive that he and his disciples 'did not even have a chance to eat' (Mark 6:31). Jesus, in the full power of his ministry, had been a number one A-list celebrity, so why was the mood changing against him in our passage? What had Jesus said to make his disciples grumble?

To discover what was happening, we need to look at the backstory, and we need to go way back into the time of Moses and the books of Exodus, Leviticus and Deuteronomy. Fundamental to all Jewish teaching was that God created life; therefore, all life was sacred, and life was symbolized by blood. Accordingly, God had given Moses laws forbidding his people to eat this sacred lifeforce, blood: 'This is a lasting ordinance for the generations to come, wherever you live: you must not eat any fat or any blood' (Leviticus 3:17; see also Deuteronomy 12:23).

Jesus was teaching in the Capernaum synagogue (John 6:59). It was a place of learning and debate and, as Jesus' Galilean base, a stronghold of his supporters. Jesus said, 'What if you see the Son of Man ascend to where he was before!' (v. 62), which confused the people even more. Was this an indication of going back, 'ascending' to Jerusalem, or was it another messianic claim that he would return to God? These people in Capernaum knew Jesus as Joseph's son from Nazareth, the carpenter; they knew his mother and brothers; so how could he speak such blasphemy? They all knew that blasphemy was punishable by death (Leviticus 24:10–16) and it would have been natural for them to want to distance themselves from such teaching, for their own (and their family's) safety.

I once heard a Russian Christian giving his testimony. His parents had never told him that his grandfather was a priest, for fear of government reprisals. At university, however, Pavel met members of a house church and heard about Jesus for the first time. Just before his finals, his Christian group was discovered by the Principal, who offered them a choice. Either they could renounce their faith in Jesus and obtain a degree or they could leave the university immediately. A couple of the young men could not face letting down their family by jeopardizing their future careers, and they chose to deny their Lord. Pavel stood firm and left university. He chose Christ before the world.

Thankfully, few of us are ever faced with such a brutal decision. Maybe our choices are far more subtle—having heard the teaching of Jesus, we make our own decision. Is it all too much trouble to become a follower? Are we content merely to hear his teaching but not let it penetrate our hearts and change our lives? Or have we faith deep enough to withstand mockery, persecution and rejection?

As well as knowing the prohibition on eating blood, every Jew grew up familiar with the story of the exodus, how Moses led the Israelites out of slavery in Egypt and how, as they wandered in the wilderness, the Lord God provided them with manna every morning (see Exodus 16:4).

There is one last piece of the background jigsaw to note before we return to John's Gospel. When God first appeared to Moses in the burning bush (Exodus 3:1–15), Moses dared to ask God's name. The reply was, 'I AM WHO I AM' (v. 14). Bearing in mind all these different trains of thought, let's see what Jesus had been saying to the eager and wondering crowd that so many found impossible to accept:

'I tell you the truth, it is not Moses who has given you the bread from heaven, but it is my Father who gives you the true bread from heaven. For the bread of God is he who comes down from heaven and gives life to the world… I am the bread of life… I tell you the truth, unless you eat the flesh of the Son of Man and drink his blood, you have no life in you… Your ancestors ate manna and died, but whoever feeds on this bread will live for ever.'
JOHN 6:32–33, 35, 53, 58

This was theological dynamite and, at the same time, repulsive, blasphemous and mindblowing. It couldn't possibly be true! When we remember where Jesus' listeners were coming from in terms of belief, it prompts us to regard them with a degree of sympathy, and we can understand better why so many genuine disciples turned away from Jesus at this point. They simply could not grasp what he was teaching, nor could they contemplate a greater authority than Moses. Perhaps they were so offended by his words that they didn't even try to get their heads around the idea.

Jesus turns to his twelve closest followers and asks the poignant question: 'You do not want to leave too, do you?' (v. 67). It's as if the crowds have melted away and Jesus' friends are left staring uncomfortably at the ground. Then Simon Peter plays his team captain role and rallies their resolve. He replies, 'Lord, to whom shall we go? You have the words of eternal life. We believe and know that you are the Holy One of God' (vv. 68–69).

Some time ago, I came across a quotation from Mark Twain: 'It ain't those parts of the Bible that I can't understand that bother me, it's the parts that I do understand.' This is a case in point. People heard Jesus' teaching but what they understood of it caused them tremendous problems. How could anyone possibly presume to supplant the mighty Moses? And was this strange man really inviting them to try cannibalism?

The whole purpose behind each Gospel was to tell the world that Jesus was different from any prophet or leader before him. He was the Holy One of God, the promised Messiah. His revolutionary teaching has always offended, disturbed and provoked questions but it has also inspired and enabled believers to find purpose and hope beyond their own understanding.

Today we have so many Bible translations, commentaries, books, daily Bible notes, videos and DVDs, all bearing witness to the life-changing words of Jesus and enabling us to understand his challenge to us as individuals. The worldwide Christian family is growing by the hour. For those of us in places where Christianity is a minority part of society, however, there are great temptations to turn away.

Jesus stands beside you as you wrestle with your thoughts: 'You do not want to leave too, do you?' Jesus is asking *you*. Maybe, deep down inside, you do want to leave. If you decide to stay, however, do you know why? Are you ready to change comfortable patterns of lifestyle and thinking? Are you willing to stay and accept the challenge, recognizing that only Jesus can feed the hunger of your soul, that only Jesus is the true and living bread? John portrays a Jesus who knows people's hearts: he knows exactly where they stand.

Consider the touching contrast between Jesus, Son of God, sent to redeem the world, and the human Jesus whose supporters are turning against him. It's virtually impossible for us to leap two thousand years back into the mindset of Jesus' time but we can be certain that he was spiritualizing the essence of his message. Jesus offered himself as the true and living bread, the bread of life (v. 35), and in verse 63, he makes it plain: 'The words I have spoken to you are spirit and they are life.'

Of course, this staggering teaching culminates in the spiritual mystery and miracle of our Holy Communion or eucharist, instituted by Jesus at the last supper (1 Corinthians 11:23–26). By eating and drinking the bread and the wine, the representations of his body and blood, we absorb the very nature of Christ, and by faith we ingest the new life he came to bring. We share this holy meal because Jesus instructed his followers to do so, and we are his followers today.

Can we even think of turning our back on the Christ who offers us everlasting life?

One Saturday, I stood at the supermarket checkout with a bag of runner beans. The young girl on the till squinted at my beans and asked, 'What are those?' When I told her they were gorgeous runner beans, her immediate reply was, 'Oh, I don't like them!' I feel that this is the attitude of the great majority towards Christianity: people don't know anything about it, they've never seen it, and it's easier to dismiss it as something they don't like than to take time to explore the challenging teaching of Jesus. And his teaching is challenging. It's a teaching that makes demands on our morality, our integrity, our possessions, our money, indeed the whole of our lives.

For reflection

Jesus, to your table led,
Now let every heart be fed
With the true and living Bread.
When we taste the mystic wine,
Of your outpoured blood the sign,
Fill our hearts with love divine.
From the bonds of sin release;
Cold and wavering faith increase;
Grant us, Lamb of God, your peace.
R.H. BAYNES (1831–95)

Prayer

Lord Jesus Christ, I do believe. Help me through my doubts and waverings. Give me courage, grace and perseverance. I do not want to leave you, now or ever. Amen

Chapter 8

'Who do you say I am?'

When Jesus came to the region of Caesarea Philippi, he asked his disciples, 'Who do people say the Son of Man is?' They replied, 'Some say John the Baptist; others say Elijah; and still others, Jeremiah or one of the prophets.' 'But what about you?' he asked. 'Who do you say I am?' Simon Peter answered, 'You are the Christ, the Son of the living God.' ... From that time on Jesus began to explain to his disciples that he must go to Jerusalem and suffer many things at the hands of the elders, chief priests and teachers of the law, and that he must be killed and on the third day be raised to life.

MATTHEW 16:13–16, 21

Jesus and the disciples had walked north from Capernaum and the Sea of Galilee up into the foothills of Mount Hermon. Today, this area of Caesarea Philippi is known as Banias and is preserved as a national park, an area of outstanding interest for all nature lovers and conservationists. There is no sign of the ancient city now but there are fragments of former pagan worship sites still visible. Somewhere in the shade of this wooded area, and quite possibly by the cool waters of the River Jordan, Jesus rested with his disciples. Their minds were no doubt still full of the mighty events of the past few weeks, talking about the beheading of John the Baptist, the feeding of the five thousand, Jesus walking on the water and the faith of the Canaanite woman whose daughter was healed. Then Jesus turns to them with this penetrating question: 'Who do people say I am?'

When we look at the replies that the disciples gave to Jesus, we get a stark reminder of the 2000-year barrier between us and them. We tend to describe people by what they are rather than who they are, such as Danny the postman, Alan the retired banker, Judith the teacher. We certainly don't trawl history in the supposition that someone has come back to life.

Although, to our ears, the disciples' replies to Jesus were distinctly weird, they were simply responding as devoutly religious men, drawing on their knowledge of scripture. The signs and wonders they had witnessed and the revolutionary teaching they had heard put Jesus beyond the realms of ordinary human experience. At the very least, he had to be a prophet. They may have had in mind Moses' words in Deuteronomy 18:15: 'The Lord your God will raise up for you a prophet like me from among your own brothers. You must listen to him.'

The mention of John the Baptist indicates what an impact this prophet had made on the people. John had called the people to repentance—literally, to turn back to worship God. We so often look at this man only as the forerunner of Jesus, and, after the account of Jesus' baptism by John in the Jordan (Matthew 3:13–17), John tends to fade from our consciousness. But remember, Jesus said there had been no one 'greater than John the Baptist' (11:11). This comment alone shows us how vivid his memory remained in the days following his murder.

In similar fashion, the mention of Elijah brings to mind the most famous and dramatic of prophets, who performed miracles and defeated the power of the priests of Baal through the power of the God of Israel. Even his death was miraculous: 2 Kings 2:11–12 tells how Elijah was taken up to heaven amid fire and wind, a testament to God's presence. The prophet Malachi had suggested a 'second coming' of Elijah, which may have prompted the disciples' comment to Jesus. 'See, I will send you the prophet Elijah before that great and dreadful day of the Lord comes,' says Malachi 4:5.

Jeremiah, on the other hand, lived much later than Elijah. Although no specific miracles were attributed to him, he was instrumental in the great spiritual reformation under King Josiah (see

2 Chronicles 34) and, throughout a long life, he served as God's faithful messenger in the face of much opposition and persecution.

In the light of these holy writings, we begin to see how the disciples came to say what they did. They were merely voicing what they had been taught and what they genuinely longed to witness. The Gospels make it clear that there was a tremendous amount of speculation about Jesus of Nazareth. Even Herod was anxious to know more about him (Luke 9:7–9). Sincere people believed that, in accepting Jesus as their Lord, they were witnesses to the power of God being made known among his people. Equally sincere people looked on his teaching as dangerous blasphemy.

Probably, the majority hadn't a clue what was going on but enjoyed the novelty of a new prophet. The disciples fell back on scripture but, when they could no longer hide behind what other people were saying, I imagine there was an embarrassed little pause. Did Jesus look at each disciple in turn as he waited for their answer? Simon Peter broke that silence as he blurted out what was in his heart: 'You are the Christ, the Son of the living God.'

In this statement, Peter makes a quantum leap, making sense of his experiences with Jesus, experiences that were to open his heart to God's purposes for the future. It was a watershed moment for him.

When the Gospels came to be written, their authors were in no doubt that Jesus was truly the Christ, the Son of the living God. With the hindsight of the resurrection and the empowerment of the Holy Spirit at Pentecost, they wrote with the zeal and confidence of missionaries. But this was a realization that came through their shared experiences as they journeyed with Jesus and then witnessed his suffering and death. They plumbed the depths of hell on earth before they recognized Jesus for who he was and began to understand his teaching.

Now it's our turn to reflect on this question from Jesus: 'Who do you say I am?' What do you think? Was Jesus just a good man or was he more than that? What do we know about him? For most people, Jesus is a collage impression made up of bits and scraps collected over the years. We have absorbed from so many different areas—Bible pictures, school assemblies, Sunday school, sermons and perhaps films such as *Who is Jesus?* or *The Passion of the Christ*. How authentic is our pastiche? Have we ever tried to find Jesus for ourselves?

Mike didn't know what to say when his twelve-year-old son came home from school and announced that he wanted to be baptized. None of the rest of the family ever went to church but the boy insisted that he wanted to attend their nearest church and be baptized. Mike felt he could handle this new fad by giving it a year at most and offering to accompany his son to church. (Having Dad in tow was bound to be a turn-off!)

The next Sunday, Mike and his son turned up for church. The vicar was somewhat bemused when Mike told him that he wasn't 'a church person' and he was just there to see what his son was on about. Father and son continued to attend the services and, after a couple of months, the two younger children clamoured to be included. Then came the day when Mike spoke to the vicar after the service and beamed, 'At last, Jesus is real to me!' A year later, when the boy was baptized, his father stood beside him to receive baptism himself. In the congregation were all the family—wife, younger children, grandparents from both sides—and friends. Mike and his son had looked for Jesus and come to know him as their Saviour.

Studying the Bible with commentaries, prayer and discussion with other Christians can all help us grow in a relationship with Jesus, and it doesn't matter how young or how old we are. God said through the prophet Jeremiah, 'You will seek me and find me when you seek me with all your heart' (29:13) and a verse in Hebrews tells us that 'Jesus Christ is the same yesterday, today and forever' (13:8). Jesus, the human face of God, is the reality of love that enables, ennobles and inspires people to live and work towards a better world.

Throughout the gospels, we see that no one who came to know Jesus was the same again. Yet many, perhaps the majority of people, never made the effort to understand who he was or how and why he suffered and was crucified. Many of them would have called themselves religious but they never made the breakthrough necessary to know Jesus for themselves.

Gwen was in her 80s when I knew her. She loved her Bible studies and said to me once, 'If only I could have asked questions 70 years ago!' Don't leave it too late to ask your own questions, and don't leave it too late to answer Jesus' question: 'Who do you say I am?'

For reflection

[Christ] is the image of the invisible God, the firstborn over all creation. For by him all things were created: things in heaven and on earth, visible and invisible… all things were created by him and for him. He is before all things, and in him all things hold together. And he is the head of the body, the church; he is the beginning and the firstborn from among the dead, so that in everything he might have supremacy. For God was pleased to have all his fullness dwell in him, and through him to reconcile to himself all things, whether things on earth or things in heaven, by making peace through his blood, shed on the cross.
COLOSSIANS 1:15–20

Chapter 9

'Can the blind lead the blind?'

[Jesus] also told them this parable: 'Can the blind lead the blind? Will they not both fall into a pit? Students are not above their teacher, but all who are fully trained will be like their teacher. Why do you look at the speck of sawdust in someone else's eye and pay no attention to the plank in your own eye? How can you say, "Friend, let me take the speck out of your eye," when you yourself fail to see the plank in your own eye? You hypocrite, first take the plank out of your eye, and then you will see clearly to remove the speck from the other person's eye.'
LUKE 6:39–42

For 30 years I lived in a Cornish town where memories ran deep. Stories were told against local worthies to make the point that although they may have given themselves airs and graces, they were as prone to double standards as anyone else. One such story, handed down from the early days of the 20th century, before the First World War, was about a family who regarded themselves as 'pillars' of their local chapel.

Such was their piety that they would not allow alcohol or smoking in the house, no games could be played on Sunday, nor were the servants allowed to work on that day. The family publicly displayed nothing but the highest moral standards.

Their 'Sunday observance' enabled their servants, young village girls, to enjoy a day off to attend chapel. On the stroke of midnight, however, those servant girls had to be up and out of bed to start work on the washing. Ostensibly such good and kind people, the family behaved with great hypocrisy and lack of consideration. It did not go unnoticed; it never does.

Jesus not only noted anomalies and hypocrisy; he highlighted what he saw, and his anger was not directed towards the Pharisees alone. Our passage from Luke 6 is addressed to 'a large crowd of his disciples... and a great number of people from all over Judea, from Jerusalem, and from the coast of Tyre and Sidon' (v. 17). When Jesus preached, he used the rabbinical method of exaggeration to wonderful effect. Pictorial exaggeration softened a jibe with humour while at the same time making the comment far more memorable. A modern-day (non-rabbinical) example is from one of my friends, who had regular battles with her teenage son in an attempt to bring order from the chaos of his bedroom. My friend despaired that he was 'knee-deep' in dirty socks, fizzy drink cans and crisp packets. Untidy the boy undoubtedly was, but we all enjoyed her flamboyant expression, even if it was coloured by exasperation. Somehow our laughter seemed to bring the situation back into proportion. In the same way, Jesus brought humour and exaggeration into his teaching.

Let's think for a moment of some of his other visual phrases:

- 'Neither do people light a lamp and put it under a bowl' (Matthew 5:15).
- 'The eye is the lamp of the body' (Matthew 6:22).
- 'You strain out a gnat but swallow a camel' (Matthew 23:24).
- 'You snakes! You brood of vipers!' (Matthew 23:33).
- 'Everyone will be salted with fire' (Mark 9:49).
- (Probably the most famous of all) 'It is easier for a camel to go through the eye of a needle than for the rich to enter the kingdom of God' (Mark 10:25).

Visual language is easy to remember and therefore, in a culture of oral teaching, easy to repeat. Except in his classic parables, Jesus used a teaching method called *charaz* in Hebrew, which meant 'stringing beads' (we might call them 'pearls of wisdom'). Even in the days of Jesus, rabbis felt that to linger too long on a subject was to lose the interest of their listeners and disciples, so they taught with the equivalent of our 'soundbites'. We tend to think that people in our time have got out of the habit of listening for long periods, but it seems that humans never have been very good at it.

In the short portion of Luke's Gospel quoted at the beginning of this chapter, we discover soundbites from Jesus on how to live together in justice and harmony. They are not mere legal statutes for law-abiding citizens, however; they are standards of the heart, ways of living to ensure each other's highest good without pretence or self-serving. Jesus did not teach rules of duty but the rules of love, and we can only truly live in this way when we genuinely want to abide by his teaching. We could slap a headline on these verses and call them 'Christian ethics', but they also contain stern warnings veiled in *charaz*. If we are not sure of what is right, how can we help another? In fact, if we cannot 'see' how to live together in this world, both internationally and individually, we are heading for disaster.

Jesus posed the rhetorical question: 'Can the blind lead the blind?' His disciples knew the answer—an emphatic 'No!' 'The blind leading the blind' has passed into our language as a graphic illustration of people, at best, going nowhere; at worst, doomed to catastrophe. Just as in the days of Jesus, if anyone remains 'blind' to this teaching, it is a blindness not of disadvantage but of choice.

At the beginning of his ministry, when Jesus read from the scroll of Isaiah in his home town synagogue at Nazareth, he spelt out his manifesto: 'The Spirit of the Lord is on me, because he has anointed me to preach good news to the poor. He has sent me to proclaim freedom for the prisoners, and recovery of sight for the blind' (Luke 4:18; see also vv. 14–21). He had come to fulfil the prophecy: he had come to set people free and to give them back their spiritual sight.

The question 'Can the blind lead the blind?' was one of several questions that Jesus put to 'a large crowd of his disciples' (Luke 6:17). Each question was a challenge for the people to recognize their lack of humility and spiritual vision. Once more, Jesus used visual humour with his disciples to drive home the message: they needed to get their attitudes sorted. After all, how could people expect to lead others when they themselves could not 'see' what they were doing? With humorous exaggeration, Jesus made the contrast between the speck of sawdust and a dirty great plank, but in the absurdity his point was made.

I remember an old saying: 'There's none so blind as those who will not see!' This was so true of those who heard Jesus' teaching but refused to see the implications for their own lives.

In his ministry, Jesus gave sight to the physically as well as the spiritually blind. Mark records a blind man being brought to Jesus at Bethsaida (8:22–26). The man's friends begged Jesus to touch him—in other words, to restore him to being an independent, useful member of the community. A blind man could not travel unaided: he was destined to poverty and begging. I love the picture of Jesus leading this man by the hand (v. 23)—a touching tenderness before the miracle of healing. Suddenly, he saw everything clearly: his eyes were opened.

Now suppose you hear Jesus ask you this same question, 'Can the blind lead the blind?' Can we be confident that we are different from that crowd of disciples, or do we have the uneasy feeling that, yes, we do have our 'blind spots', especially when it comes to our own faults and the shortcomings of those we love. Pride, jealousy, ambition, insecurity—all these emotions are very good at creating 'planks' in our eyes, which become obstacles to happy relationships with people. We, too, may need healing.

How should we go about letting Jesus heal our spiritual blindness? There is so much going on in our world, so much noise, so many people clamouring to be seen and heard, and we can talk all day long without really listening to or seeing anyone. Perhaps we need to take more time to look and listen, to disentangle ourselves from the centre of a universe of our own making. We need to listen to God and open our eyes to what Jesus did and taught; we need to listen to the needs of others instead of deafening them with our own solutions; we need to create space and silence for prayer and confession. Then we can experience Jesus' healing touch.

Losing our blindness means realizing that no one is perfect, least of all ourselves. Jesus shows us the futility of interfering in other people's lives before we have straightened out our own—and he knows that sometimes it feels far more satisfying to be 'blind' to our own shortcomings.

A penetrating sentence from John's letter hits me right between the eyes: 'If we claim to be without sin, we deceive ourselves' (1 John 1:8). But then comes the wonderful assurance as John points us in the direction of forgiveness and healing: 'If we confess our sins, he is faithful and just and will forgive us our sins and purify us from all unrighteousness' (v. 9). Once we have taken that long, honest look at our sin, there is no need to be overwhelmed or despairing. Through Jesus, God waits for us to confess that we have fallen short of his standard, and we can receive his forgiveness. It's a fresh start—and when we keep our eyes on Jesus, then we will be used in God's service, right where we are.

For reflection

The 18th-century hymn writer John Newton had been involved in the transatlantic slave trade for several years, but came to bitterly regret that part of his life. This fact gives greater weight to the meaning of his much-loved words:

Amazing grace, how sweet the sound
that saved a wretch like me!
I once was lost, but now am found,
was blind but now I see.

Prayer

Lord, open my eyes that I may know your saving grace.

Chapter 10

'Do you see this woman?'

'Two men owed money to a certain moneylender. One owed him five hundred denarii, and the other fifty. Neither of them had the money to pay him back, so he cancelled the debts of both. Now which of them will love him more?' Simon replied, 'I suppose the one who had the bigger debt cancelled.' 'You have judged correctly,' Jesus said. Then he turned toward the woman and said to Simon, 'Do you see this woman? I came into your house. You did not give me any water for my feet, but she wet my feet with her tears and wiped them with her hair. You did not give me a kiss, but this woman, from the time I entered, has not stopped kissing my feet. You did not put oil on my head, but she has poured perfume on my feet. Therefore, I tell you, her many sins have been forgiven.'

LUKE 7:41–47

The verses immediately before this parable describe how an unnamed woman anointed Jesus with expensive perfume. In our mind's eye, let us enter this scene, in which Jesus has accepted an invitation to a Pharisee's home for a meal. Everything is going well until this woman with a dubious past comes and starts sobbing on Jesus' feet. The distraught woman's sorrow pours out in a torrent of tears until Jesus' feet become soaked. It is then that the unthinkable happens: she lets down her hair and wipes his feet dry before anointing them with precious scent. Simon, the host Pharisee, is appalled. Luke writes that he condemns Jesus and the woman 'to himself' (v. 39), but he obviously makes no attempt to hide his disgust.

Simon's disgust was directed to the woman and also to Jesus, who, in his view, should not have accepted such extreme gestures from such a disreputable woman. Jesus, however, was not repelled by the woman or her actions. He received her sorrow and was unembarrassed by her devotion. While the rest of the company were scandalized, he alone accepted her sincerity.

We find this story, with slight differences, in all four Gospels, which gives us an inkling of what a momentous event it was. Why should the woman's anointing of Jesus feature so prominently in the disciples' memory over and above, say, the parable of the good Samaritan or the last words of Jesus before his ascension (which only Luke records)?

Matthew (26:6–7) and Mark (14:3) record the host as Simon the leper and describe the woman pouring expensive perfume over Jesus' head. Luke and John specify the woman's copious weeping and say that she poured the perfume over his feet, but only John names her as Mary, sister to Martha and Lazarus (John 12:3). It is a beautiful Gospel story that portrays Jesus' accessibility and forgiveness. Each individual was important and a genuine approach to him was met with compassion. It is also a declaration of Jesus' divine nature and his authority to forgive sins, which was a major stumbling block to the Jewish religious leaders.

Just imagine the tension mounting in the room as the woman used her loose hair as a towel to wipe Jesus' feet. It was an extraordinarily intimate gesture! Here was a woman lavishing attention on a man—not her husband—brazenly violating all social convention. A woman could untie her hair only for her husband, and it was considered humiliating to touch feet—a job left for the lowest servant. Nevertheless, this woman, distracted by her guilt and grief, anointed Jesus both physically and emotionally from her heart.

Simon was inwardly squirming for another reason, however. As host, he had committed certain social gaffes, which Jesus proceeded to point out. Guests expected to be offered water to wash and refresh their feet, and in Middle Eastern etiquette the host normally gave a kiss of greeting. A little oil poured on the head acted like water for the feet, soothing in the heat. These were small things in themselves but essential courtesies in those times. Perhaps Simon had left the water and oil to his servants to attend to. Whatever the circumstances, however, he was a Pharisee and, with his religious status and financial advantage, he should have been a better host.

Simon the Pharisee had nothing but contempt for this woman, and it was to this stiff-necked, self-righteous attitude that Jesus addressed his parable. The laws of Moses laid down moral codes which ensured that people who found themselves in debt were not exploited. However, cancellation of debt was at the discretion of the lender. Simon could not avoid the correct answer to Jesus' first question: 'Which of them will love him more?' Nor could he avoid the question that nobody expected Jesus to ask: 'Do you see this woman?'

If all the local people knew about her life (and 'sinful' is a strong adjective), it is hard to believe that no one had noticed her moving towards the table where Jesus was reclining. Were there so many guests that, until she began to weep on Jesus' feet, she had appeared to be one of the extra servants hired for the party? It would seem apparent that Simon the Pharisee had not noticed the woman in his home, otherwise he would certainly have had her thrown out. The disciples must have seen her but were probably doing everything possible to ignore her. After all, if they knew what sort of woman she was, they would all have felt that she had no business to be in their master's company.

Matthew, Mark and John place this event at Bethany, the village on the other side of the Mount of Olives from Jerusalem, the home of Jesus' close friends Mary, Martha and Lazarus. In the earlier verses of Luke's account, we are given an insight into Jesus' social life (vv. 34, 36); obviously he enjoyed convivial meals with a variety of people. Some would have been offering the charismatic rabbi genuine hospitality while others would have made their invitation for more devious reasons. A wealthy Pharisee's house would have included an open courtyard where, on warm evenings, guests met to share his hospitality. The courtyard would have been open to uninvited guests, villagers and passers-by, who could hover around listening to the principal visitors. We need to keep reminding ourselves that these people's lives were lived 'in community', and a meal like this would have been both private entertainment and a focus for public curiosity.

Many Pharisees mistrusted Jesus at best and, at worst, planned to trick him into incriminating himself (Matthew 22:15; Luke 11:53–54). While this does not seem to be the case here, Simon was affronted that Jesus allowed the woman to show such intimate devotion to him, and convinced himself that Jesus was no man of God. To Simon's way of thinking, Jesus had inexplicably elevated the undesirable woman's actions above his own hospitality. He may have been bewildered but he couldn't miss the point of Jesus' mini-parable about the two men who owed money. Obviously the person who owed the most would be the most relieved and grateful. But then Simon saw his dinner party heading for disaster when Jesus suddenly spoke the words, 'her many sins have been forgiven' (v. 47). If anyone there was gathering evidence against Jesus, then this was the jackpot: blasphemy! Simon and everyone else listening would have gasped in disbelief. Human beings could not forgive sins; that was the sole prerogative of almighty God.

Whatever sins this woman had committed, she came to Jesus in deep sorrow. In that culture, when a death occurred, the family would hire mourners to weep and wail over the body in a display of respect and affection. Sometimes the mourners' tears were collected and stored in special glass containers called 'tear-cups'. This woman, however, had so much accumulated grief—too much to be contained in a small glass jar—that her tears streamed down on to Jesus' feet. She probably expected to be sent away but, to her joy, Jesus accepted her and her gift of perfume without a word of condemnation.

Jesus never rejects us. This is where we realize the vast gulf between the way we treat people—how our prejudices and judgments colour our attitude to others—and the way God treats them.

I close my eyes and imagine Jesus asking me the question: 'Do you see this woman?' Before I can reply, I have to ask myself to be honest: do I want to see? I can think of plenty of women today whom society shuns because of their behaviour. Think how you would react if your birthday party was gatecrashed by a heroin addict. Could you include on your family holiday a teenager convicted of a mugging? It is so easy to condemn people, rejecting them out of hand—but Jesus does not, and his followers must not.

If we all treated other people with the love that Jesus showed to the woman, accepting rather than judging, acting with welcome rather than contempt, with understanding instead of condemnation, just think how our communities would be transformed. Instead of the sour odour of scorn or indifference, we would live in the fresh scent of compassion and respect. We might even get close to obeying Jesus' teaching: 'A new command I give you: love one another. As I have loved you, so you must love one another' (John 13:34). This is not the rambling of an ancient, well-meaning eccentric; it is the living, life-transforming word of the Son of God. We need to open our eyes and, in the power of the Holy Spirit, reevaluate what we 'see'. Whoever the woman was who wept over Jesus' feet, the memory of her humble act of love has been told wherever the Gospel is heard.

Prayer

Lord God, give me grace and humility to welcome in your name the outcast, the neglected, the isolated and forgotten, the annoying and the unlovable. Help me to realize how much I have been forgiven so that I may meet others as my brothers and sisters in you.

Chapter 11

'What did Moses command you?'

Jesus then left that place and went into the region of Judea and across the Jordan. Again crowds of people came to him, and as was his custom, he taught them. Some Pharisees came and tested him by asking, 'Is it lawful for a man to divorce his wife?' 'What did Moses command you?' he replied. They said, 'Moses permitted a man to write a certificate of divorce and send her away.' 'It was because your hearts were hard that Moses wrote you this law,' Jesus replied. 'But at the beginning of creation God "made them male and female". "For this reason a man will leave his father and mother and be united to his wife, and the two will become one flesh." So they are no longer two, but one. Therefore what God has joined together, let no one separate.'
MARK 10:1–9

I was asked once to talk about 'marriage in a Christian context' with 14- and 15-year-old pupils at a London school. A streetwise youth shot up a gangling arm with the first question: 'How much does it cost to get divorced, Miss?' It left me with the distinct impression that this young man was so indoctrinated by our finance-driven culture that the cheaper option—on anything—was to be preferred. More probably, he had lived or was living through his parents' divorce, so that this question was first on his mind. But let's return to first-century Judea, for it seems that divorce was also uppermost in the minds of the Pharisees who went to question Jesus of Nazareth.

Amazing events had taken place over the previous few weeks for Jesus and his disciples. They'd travelled north from Galilee as far as Caesarea Philippi, where Peter had made his declaration, 'You are the Christ!' Then they'd walked back down over the hills of the Golan, returning to the town that Jesus had made his home base, Capernaum. Now, in these first verses of Mark 10, we find that Jesus has brought his disciples away from the Sea of Galilee, south along the Jordan valley and up into Judea on the way to Jerusalem.

In Luke 9:52 we read, 'And he sent messengers on ahead... to get things ready for him.' This gives us an insight into how Jesus and his disciples travelled around, and how his ministry operated without any of the means of communication at the disposal of today's preachers. News spread as to what Jesus was doing and where he would be staying, and the crowds followed.

In Mark 10, along come a group of Pharisees, delighted to have a chance to manipulate Jesus into incriminating himself. These ultra-religious, learned men were more than irritated by Jesus' teaching and popularity: he was undermining their authority before their own people. Of course, Jesus knew full well that many were seeking to destroy him, and we read his strong words to the religious authorities in John 8:37: 'You are ready to kill me, because you have no room for my word.'

Let's picture the scene depicted in our passage from Mark's Gospel. It was 'his custom' to teach the crowds, who would have consisted not only of those living in the village but also, as we have seen before, of many who had come from miles away. There would have been many good venues for Jesus to teach in—a synagogue, either inside it or in the shade of the building, or in the middle of the village.

The waiting Pharisees were feeling superior. They had chosen an ace for their opening question: 'Is it lawful for a man to divorce his wife?' In an instant the atmosphere would have changed from happy anticipation to frozen silence as the people waited for Jesus' response.

In those days, divorce was a hot topic between two rabbinic schools of thought. The school of Shammai interpreted the laws as stating that divorce was permissible only for adultery (the woman's, of course). Meanwhile, the school of Hillel stretched their interpretation so widely that they taught that divorce was possible if the wife merely spoiled the evening meal. How would Jesus answer? What school of thought would he follow?

At this point, I think we need to take a look at what marriage involved in the Middle East of the first century. Families lived in clusters in close proximity to their relatives—very much as an extended family. Marriages were usually arranged by fathers even before the children reached puberty, and the girl-wife would automatically go to live in her husband's family home. This home would include her new in-laws, any of her husband's unmarried siblings and, often, other sons' wives and children. Because of the emphasis on kinship, there was a high percentage of intermarriage within the family tribe, even between cousins, but polygamy was rare. By the time of Jesus, monogamy had become the norm, with concepts of 'honour', 'purity', 'commitment' and 'responsibility' cementing society. The birth of a son was usually necessary, however, before a new wife's place in the household was truly assured.

At least, that was the theory. The practice, as all societies have discovered, was very different. The very fact that Moses had found it necessary to make provision for divorce (Deuteronomy 24:1–3) indicates an underlying current of hurt and humiliation, creating the need to find the least harmful domestic solution.

In the mind and heart of every Jew, there was no greater prophet of the Lord than Moses. He was the channel of God's law, the hero who had led the people out of slavery in Egypt, and any pronouncement attributed to Moses was immutable—immutable, but open to selective rabbinical interpretation.

Jesus knew perfectly well what Moses had written, but he sidestepped this emotive argument on divorce to turn the focus towards God's original purpose for marriage. It was a dangerous thing, tantamount to blasphemy, to supplant Moses, but the Pharisees could not argue when Jesus referred to a higher power than Moses—the power of God, the Lord God of Abraham, Isaac and

Israel. Nevertheless, there seems to be a distinct echo here of the formula 'You have heard that it was said... but I tell you...' (Matthew 5:38–39). Jesus was speaking with the authority of God himself.

Jesus asked the Pharisees to recall what Moses had commanded, to make the point that the law offered a compromise, causing the least possible disruption to family groups. As the people emerged from slavery and the years of wandering in the desert, a paramount consideration had to be the preservation of blood-ties for family stability. Marriage became a solemn blood relationship and binding covenant, even the symbol of the relationship between God and his people (Genesis 17:1–7; Jeremiah 31:31–34; 1 Corinthians 11:23–25; Hebrews 8).

The men and women watching Jesus with the Pharisees would have had all these ideas going though their minds, but before he could be accused of blasphemy, Jesus guided them to God's original purpose. He reminded them that God created the world and everything in it, with men and women as part of that creation. God's purpose was for caring, mutual support and the strengthening of the community. The ideal of marriage was a great blessing to all. The Pharisees had lost sight of God in their discussions; they had become occupied with marital failure and blame instead of rejoicing in the interdependence of a loving union. Jesus made them think again.

He made it perfectly clear to his listeners that he had come not to abolish the law but to fulfil it (Matthew 5:17). It was difficult, however, for the people to grasp that Jesus takes God's law further —away from the strict letter into the loving spirit at the heart of the law. And this is where we connect to the story. We need to know God's law, too.

The commands that God gave through Moses at Mount Sinai (the Ten Commandments: see Exodus 20:1–17) first and foremost lifted people's hearts to worship God. Next followed a law about duties to parents, and then the 'negative commands' ('You shall not murder', and so on) by which so many cultures still stand.

They are rules for living together in harmony, whether in family groups or on a broader, international scale.

These ancient laws spelt out a moral framework for the Israelites, marking them out as distinct from all other nations because of their covenant relationship with the Lord God. Notice how each commandment is about relationships—with God, with our parents and then with the wider community. The stipulations for right living are intended to enhance good relationships, to bring about justice, peace and prosperity, or (to jump ahead to New Testament terms) the kingdom of heaven. Breaking these rules for living has consequences, which ripple inexorably into the lives of those around us—parents, children, extended family and friends.

In asking us the question 'What did Moses command you?' Jesus is opening our eyes to more than legal requirements. He is reminding us that laws are given because of our hardness of heart. We may keep the letter of the law but ignore the deeper purpose behind it. Yes, marriage is a solemn covenant, but the sad truth is that once trust between two people has broken down, their relationship has ended long before a piece of paper can be issued to dissolve the marriage legally.

The apostle Paul was proud of being a Pharisee and was as steeped in the law as anyone could be, yet in his letter to the believers in Rome he wrote, 'But now, by dying to what once bound us, we have been released from the law so that we serve in the new way of the Spirit, and not in the old way of the written code' (Romans 7:6). Unlike the Gospel writers, who recorded relatively short teachings of Jesus, Paul had time in his letters to follow through the train of thought regarding the law and the Spirit. We are not called to be legalistic automata; we are called by Jesus to live by the law of love.

In another letter, Paul wrote, 'So the law was put in charge to lead us to Christ that we might be justified by faith. Now that faith has come, we are no longer under the supervision of the law' (Galatians 3:24–25). In Jesus Christ we can move from the sins of the past to a new beginning motivated by our response to his love and sacrifice. God spoke through Moses to give the people of Israel commandments for life, and Jesus himself commended these laws to the ruler who was seeking eternal life (Luke 18:18–20). They will always be the foundation, but, through faith in Jesus as Lord and Saviour, love has replaced fear in the new order of his eternal reign.

For reflection

Why not prayerfully read through the Ten Commandments again and ask God to open your eyes to the consequences of breaking his laws? Then use these words from Psalm 119:10–15 to make your response to Jesus.

I seek you with all my heart;
do not let me stray from your commands.
I have hidden your word in my heart
that I might not sin against you.
Praise be to you, O Lord;
teach me your decrees.
With my lips I recount
all the laws that come from your mouth.
I will rejoice in following your statutes
as one rejoices in great riches.
I meditate on your precepts
and consider your ways.

Chapter 12

'Do you believe this?'

On his arrival, Jesus found that Lazarus had already been in the tomb for four days. Bethany was less than two miles from Jerusalem, and many Jews had come to Martha and Mary to comfort them in the loss of their brother. When Martha heard that Jesus was coming, she went out to meet him, but Mary stayed at home. 'Lord,' Martha said to Jesus, 'if you had been here, my brother would not have died. But I know that even now God will give you whatever you ask.' Jesus said to her, 'Your brother will rise again.' Martha answered, 'I know he will rise again in the resurrection at the last day.' Jesus said to her, 'I am the resurrection and the life. Those who believe in me will live, even though they die; and whoever lives and believes in me will never die. Do you believe this?' 'Yes, Lord,' she told him, 'I believe that you are the Christ, the Son of God, who was to come into the world.'
JOHN 11:17–27

On leaving school in the mid-1960s, my first job was as a reporter for the local newspaper, and one of my tasks was to attend funerals. Standing outside the church on the first of these assignments, I took names from the general public, then went back to the house for a list of family mourners. Woe betide the reporter who omitted a name from the week's obituary column! At 17, I had only experienced two funeral services, and I had never been to the 'wake' that would follow. I was in for a surprising initiation!

Soberly dressed in black—I even had a black pen—I knocked on the door with what I considered a serious 'funeral' face. My eyes popped at the table groaning under an appetizing feast for the family and close friends who had managed to cram inside the home. Neighbours were making tea and the men had sloped into the garden with glasses of much stronger liquid. In teenage indignation, I felt it was totally irreverent to munch sausage rolls, fish paste sandwiches and all manner of cakes and sponges at such a time. I collected the names of family mourners to add to the brief life sketch already gathered and escaped back to my typewriter. What a lot I had to learn about human nature!

Death is such a major event in any community that, since the first cluster groups of early humankind, death has been marked as a fundamental rite of passage. Ancient burial mounds, tombs and shrines denote the same need to register a loved one's departure as today's roadside shrines or mounds of flowers. Headstones bear emotional verses that testify to loving relationships, and obituary columns summarize a person's life in a couple of inches of type. One of the saddest things to contemplate is the unmourned death, unnoticed by anybody except, perhaps, the funeral director, the solicitor and the minister presiding over the funeral.

Our Bible passage shows Mary and Martha as they mourned over the death of Lazarus. The culture in which they lived meant that their grief was compounded: not only had their dear brother died, but their future lives as two unmarried sisters would be very difficult without a man to protect and provide for them. Worse still, their trusted friend Jesus was miles away.

Rabbi Judah, who lived AD140–165, wrote of the burial customs of the time, 'Even the poorest in Israel shall hire not less than two flutes and one wailing woman.' So it seems that the Bethany family was not in the league of 'the poorest', as John tells us that 'many Jews had come' to comfort the sisters (v. 19). Traditionally, mourners would stay at the house for seven days, until the official period of mourning was over. Interestingly, archaeologists have uncovered many ossuaries (the final resting place for skeletal remains) from around the Bethany area, bearing Galilean inscriptions. This may have been another factor in bringing Jesus to stay with Lazarus, Mary and Martha from time to time, for Jesus and his disciples may have had extended family and friends in common with them 'up north' around Galilee.

Over the centuries, Martha and Mary have become pigeon-holed, made into stereotypes. We tend to think of Martha as the busy, houseproud sister, complaining that Mary (probably the younger sister) wasn't pulling her weight. Twenty seconds of sibling spat (Luke 10:40), and they were labelled for eternity! The account in John 11 presents us with another side of Martha and Mary, enough to remind us that they, like us, cannot be judged by one aspect of their lives.

When word reached the house that Jesus was approaching, Martha dropped any domestic duties and flew to meet her Lord, leaving Mary to cope with the mourners. Martha greeted Jesus in anguish with those words we have all used—'If only...'—blurting them out in a haze of grief, confusion and recrimination. Jesus had not been there when they all needed him. She did accept, though, that despite Lazarus' death, Jesus would bring the presence of God into the situation. We can tell by her short conversation with him that she believed in resurrection, but only 'at the last day' (v. 24), at some God-appointed time in the future. Lazarus had been dead for four days by the time Jesus arrived. Rabbinic teaching stated that the soul left the body after three days, so after four days in the tomb the soul had gone. That was that.

It would seem that for Jews in Jesus' time, resurrection was a much more seriously held belief than the frustratingly sparse references in the Old Testament would suggest (Matthew 22:28; Luke 14:14). We know that the Sadducees opposed the notion of resurrection (Luke 20:27), but the Pharisees fully accepted it in some form. To the grieving, bewildered Martha, Jesus now makes a mindblowing statement: '*I am* the resurrection and the life.' Then he asks her, 'Do you believe this?'

When politicians are asked a question, they tend to devise the most intricate verbal choreography to avoid a straight answer, yes or no. Not so with this woman of Bethany: Martha replies in total faith and her reply stands among the greatest ever made to Jesus.

'Yes, Lord,' she told him, 'I believe that you are the Christ, the Son of God, who was to come into the world' (v. 27).

Let's pause for a moment and take a closer look at what Jesus was asking Martha to believe. It was one of the six monumental 'I am' statements recorded by John (6:35; 8:12; 10:7; 10:11; 15:1). In the clearest way yet, Jesus was asserting the fact that he was God. Jesus himself is life, the creation and gift of God alone. To believe in Jesus as Lord of life and conqueror of death extends the believer's mind into the mysteries of an unknown, everlasting dimension. This is the stuff of theological tomes, dissertations, academic argument and intellectual hypotheses. Nobody can be sure of the 'what', 'why', 'when' or 'how'—but we can know the 'who'.

Let's look at what Paul wrote to those new in the Christian faith in Corinth:

For since in the wisdom of God the world through its wisdom did not know him, God was pleased through the foolishness of what was preached to save those who believe. Jews demand miraculous signs and Greeks look for wisdom, but we preach Christ crucified: a stumbling block to Jews and foolishness to Gentiles, but to those whom God has called, both Jews and Greeks, Christ the power of God and the wisdom of God.

1 CORINTHIANS 1:21–24

No wonder Jesus said that we need to become like little children before we can enter the kingdom of heaven. We can't buy our way to eternal life or work out a sophisticated scientific formula to prove resurrection. All we need is a childlike trust and a complete reliance on God's grace. I expect that, proportionately, as many people now as in the time of the New Testament cannot bring themselves to believe in resurrection. It is an act not of human power but wholly of God's.

As Jesus and Martha climbed the road back up to Bethany, she made that great leap of faith, from the fears and doubts of her mind to the knowledge that her heart whispered. Yes, she did believe what Jesus her Lord had told her. This is where we have to recognize that understanding is often far removed from believing.

How would we reply if we were walking side by side with Jesus and he suddenly stopped, turned to face us and asked, 'Do *you* believe this?'

We have the advantage over Martha and Mary because we know about the events of Easter, and there is one particular phrase that comes to my mind when I tussle with the concept of resurrection. It comes from Luke's account of the crucifixion, when the penitent thief hanging on a cross beside Jesus calls out, 'Jesus, remember me when you come into your kingdom.' Jesus replies, 'I tell you the truth, today you will be with me in paradise' (Luke 23:42–43). I find this sentence a real comfort and encouragement as it implies that resurrection, or life after death, is an immediate state. Rather than being a disembodied soul kicking around in 'Sheol' (the Hebrew term for the grave) until some distant day, our hope is of being immediately 'with God'.

Many years ago, I met a retired minister, well into his 90s. He had spent his days preaching the life, death and resurrection of Jesus Christ but, at the end of his own life, and because of some tragic family events, he no longer believed in a life after death. I had to admire his honesty and candour: whatever anyone would think of him, he was not prepared to be a hypocrite.

Perversely, I would imagine that the number of people believing in some kind of afterlife is far greater than the number of Christians worldwide. Jesus' question to Martha, and to each one of us, is whether we believe that *he* is the resurrection and the life. That is quite different from a vague hope of 'something' when our physical body comes to a halt. We have to differentiate between nursing hopeful longings for what we would like to happen and being able to put our trust in the supreme power of God in Jesus Christ.

An assurance of love and joy in the risen Jesus characterizes Christian belief, from the first disciples to the present day. No one can pretend it is an easy concept, but Jesus also said, 'With God all things are possible' (Matthew 19:26). When Jesus posed the question, 'Do you believe this?' Martha answered, 'Yes'. How would you reply?

For reflection

In the 18th century, great waves of Christian revival challenged men and women to sing their faith in the poetry of hymns. One of my favourites was written by Samuel Medley (1738–99) and this version is taken from The Lutheran Hymnal *(1941).*

I know that my redeemer lives;
What comfort this sweet sentence gives!
He lives, He lives who once was dead;
He lives, my ever-living Head.

He lives and grants me daily breath;
He lives, and I shall conquer death:
He lives my mansion to prepare;
He lives to lead me safely there.

In what ways do these lines of poetry challenge or encourage your faith?

Chapter 13

'Which of these was a neighbour?'

Jesus said: 'A man was going down from Jerusalem to Jericho, when he fell into the hands of robbers. They stripped him of his clothes, beat him and went away, leaving him half dead. A priest happened to be going down the same road, and when he saw the man, he passed by on the other side. So too, a Levite, when he came to the place and saw him, passed by on the other side. But a Samaritan, as he travelled, came where the man was; and when he saw him, he took pity on him. He went to him and bandaged his wounds, pouring on oil and wine. Then he put the man on his own donkey, took him to an inn and took care of him. The next day he took out two silver coins and gave them to the innkeeper. "Look after him," he said, "and when I return, I will reimburse you for any extra expense you may have." Which of these three do you think was a neighbour to the man who fell into the hands of robbers?' The expert in the law replied, 'The one who had mercy on him.' Jesus told him, 'Go and do likewise.'

LUKE 10:30–37

Of all the parables Jesus told, this parable of the good Samaritan must rate among the top three in terms of popularity. I remember watching an audience of parents and grandparents at a Boys' Brigade display evening when a group had elected to mime a modern version of the good Samaritan. Their leader narrated the mime, the city names were changed to two local town names and the donkey became a motorbike. But the essentials of the story were unchanged: the mugging, the desperate need for help, the help withheld and rescue coming from the least likely person.

It struck me that, although we were a mixed audience of different faiths and none, the essential truth of the parable transcended our diversity and spoke to each one of us. Regardless of background, religion or age, we could all understand the meaning of this story.

Jesus told a story that challenged people to face their fears, weaknesses and prejudices. He went straight for the racial tension and religious hypocrisy of his day, leaving the lawyer who had asked the initial question about neighbours with only one possible answer. It was not the answer he wanted to give. He couldn't even repeat the detested word 'Samaritan' but he had to admit that it was the outsider who had been 'neighbour' to the man in need.

Let's pause here and explore the background to this parable. Luke was in no doubt that the lawyer was trying to be clever with Jesus: he records how the lawyer 'stood up to test Jesus' (v. 25). When he asked what he should do to inherit eternal life, it was an academic question, a theological game, and not part of a sincere quest. Jesus directed the man's thinking back to the laws of Moses, and the lawyer piously repeated words from Deuteronomy 6:5, 'Love the Lord your God with all your heart and with all your soul and with all your strength', and Leviticus 19:18, 'Love your neighbour as yourself.'

Jesus didn't prolong the hypothetical argument with this smug lawyer; instead he told this wonderful story of help from unexpected quarters.

On my first pilgrimage to the Holy Land, I stood looking down to where the old road between Jerusalem and Jericho snaked along the wadi (a deep valley in the desert). There is little more than 20 miles between the two cities but in that distance the traveller descends approximately 1200 metres. In New Testament times, the route was a notorious bandits' paradise. It was—and remains —a barren, inhospitable landscape. Any man who travelled from Jerusalem to Jericho on his own was probably asking for trouble. Maybe Jesus was implying that the attack was the man's own fault but he needed help, regardless.

Jesus chose a priest and a Levite as characters, just as we might choose a bishop or dean of a cathedral. They represented high-profile religious men whose lives were expected to be exemplary. Both priest and Levite were superior to the ordinary people in terms of education and privilege, the Levites enjoying a hereditary position as temple officials, subordinate to the priests. Their personal standards were governed by rigid adherence to the Law of Moses as well as a plethora of additional regulations, which had been added over several centuries by over-diligent experts.

In this parable, Jesus takes a swipe at the suffocating legalism that twisted otherwise good and honourable men to become hypocrites. To every Jew, life was sacred, and it should have been their instinctive response to help the victim by the roadside. Sadly, their fear of becoming unclean by touching what could have turned out to be a dead body, and their inflexible regard for rituals and duties, had robbed them of *hesed*, the uniquely Hebrew word meaning 'loving kindness'.

Jesus not only put the spotlight on men who made a mockery of true faith; he also chose to name the hero of the story as a Samaritan. To Jesus' listeners, this was truly scandalous. Samaritans had defiled their nation by intermarriage with Gentiles (see comment in Chapter 6) and were marginalized and despised by the Jews. I can imagine blank stares of incredulity and discomfort among the crowd as they heard this parable unfold. Nice drama, they were thinking, but not a realistic cast!

Rabbis taught that when scripture spoke of loving your neighbour, the neighbour in question had to mean your own people— other Jews. This fostered a religious exclusiveness that was totally contrary to the teaching of Jesus. Jewish humour is full of irony, and the irony of the parable of the good Samaritan is that when Jesus asked the Jewish lawyer which of the three characters had been a neighbour, the answer was 'the one from a neighbouring nation'.

The awesome nature of God's holy word is that, although it was written by many authors over many centuries, whoever reads it can find a relevance to their contemporary situation. This enables the reader to deepen their own relationship to God through Jesus Christ, his Son. From our vantage point in history, it's very easy to nod wisely over the parable of the good Samaritan and note the obvious points Jesus was making. I firmly believe, however, that the story was never meant to be set in history. Jesus used the teaching style of parable so that all his followers—then and now—would be encouraged to face the truth about themselves and about the challenge of walking the way of the kingdom.

What response does Jesus find in us when he asks us the question, 'Which one of these was a neighbour?'

Imagine that you have been mugged on your way home. You've been beaten to the ground and had your personal belongings and money stolen. You are paralysed with fear and blood is running from your wounds.

Now think of the person you distrust and dislike most in all the world. How would you react if it was this person who put themselves out to come to you, if theirs was the face that bent gently over you, theirs the hands that washed your body, theirs the money that arranged for your convalescence? Would you still harbour feelings of hatred for them?

The human mind is quite brilliant at self-justification, excuses and sloth. Perhaps this is why the world is in such a deplorable state: everyone knows what ought to be done but we all leave it to someone else to do. Not so in the kingdom of God. There is no room for putting ourselves in a better light, no room for resting on our own respectability or on someone else's disreputable character. When Jesus asks a question, we need to give an answer. We need to make a choice and act decisively.

Do you remember what James, the brother of Jesus, wrote in his letter to the first-century believers? The whole tenor of his letter is that genuine faith inevitably produces people who work to promote goodness, justice and truth, with self-control, prayer and encouragement as hallmarks of the Christian 'family'. Like Jesus, his brother and Lord, he attacks hypocrisy. Three verses that dig into my heart are, 'Suppose a brother or sister is without clothes and daily food. If one of you says to them, "Go, I wish you well; keep warm and well fed", but does nothing about their physical needs, what good is it? In the same way, faith by itself, if it is not accompanied by action, is dead' (James 2:15–17).

Nothing has changed in two thousand years. The eternal truth remains that when a member of the human race is hungry, dispossessed, abused or violated and needs help, we all become neighbours, called to act, to help. Maybe this is stating the obvious, but perhaps the obvious has become so familiar that we have stopped paying attention to it.

Jesus taught a different way. The parable of the good Samaritan shows how compassion and integrity break through all claims of prejudice and exclusivity. It demonstrates how an act of selfless care can bring about peace and well-being, the *shalom* of God. As you consider this story and as you listen to Jesus asking you, 'Which one of these was a neighbour?' you just might also hear the words, 'Go on, you can do the same!'

For reflection

Prayerfully consider your own opportunities for 'neighbourliness'—not just among the people who live close to you but those with whom you work, people behind supermarket checkouts, those who collect your rubbish, those sitting next to you on the train or those you meet at the school gate. Ask God to open your eyes to see the acts of neighbourliness that you could do for them.

Chapter 14

'What is the kingdom of God like?'

Then Jesus asked, 'What is the kingdom of God like? What shall I compare it to? It is like a mustard seed, which a man took and planted in his garden. It grew and became a tree, and the birds of the air perched in its branches.' Again he asked, 'What shall I compare the kingdom of God to? It is like yeast that a woman took and mixed into a large amount of flour until it worked all through the dough.'

LUKE 13:18–21

A few verses before this passage, Luke tells us that Jesus had been teaching in a synagogue. It was a sabbath and among the crowd Jesus noticed a woman who was 'bent over and could not straighten up at all' (v. 11b). When Jesus laid hands on her and healed her, the synagogue ruler and his cronies griped and criticized because Jesus had healed, and therefore 'worked', on the sabbath (v. 14)

Picture the moment. An ecstatic woman, released after 18 years from an infirmity that had ruined her life; a marvelling, adoring crowd, mesmerized by the power and authority of this travelling rabbi from Nazareth; irritated synagogue officials tut-tutting at such violation of the laws of Moses. Suddenly Jesus addresses the ruler of the synagogue and other leaders in a shout of exasperation: 'You hypocrites!' (v. 15).

What a public humiliation for the religious leaders! Can you imagine them slamming the synagogue doors after Jesus and the crowd had left?

I have a feeling that someone in the crowd had asked Jesus about the kingdom of God, and Jesus replied using the rhetorical question at the start of our passage. Maybe a man (and it would certainly have been a man, as women were not allowed to speak in synagogues) was trying to sort out in his mind why this wonderful prophet Jesus clashed so fiercely with the revered religious leaders. Surely they both followed the Law of Moses? I imagine this man drawing alongside Jesus and saying, 'Master, we don't understand what you mean when you speak of the kingdom of God. What is this kingdom of God like?'

The simplicity with which Jesus portrayed the kingdom of God made it possible for all his hearers to understand what he meant. It wasn't, however, what they expected or wanted to hear. To get a glimpse of their perplexity, we need to investigate the root of the phrase that he used.

Even as a young boy of twelve (see Luke 2:41–52), Jesus showed a deep knowledge of scripture, or what we call the 'Old Testament'. Now this is arguably not the best use of language as, in our time, anything 'old' tends to be equated with 'boring' and 'irrelevant', and is likely to be put to one side and ignored. But when we are searching for the meaning behind Jesus' teaching, and what it meant for those who first heard his words, we need to search our Bibles as a whole.

When King David praised the Lord God of Israel before the people, he used these words in his prayer: 'Yours, O Lord, is the greatness and the power and the glory and the majesty and the splendour, for everything in heaven and earth is yours. Yours, O Lord, is the kingdom; you are exalted as head over all' (1 Chronicles 29:11).

The faith of the people of Israel was in the God of all creation, to whom everything and everyone in the world was subordinate. God had created a perfect world, which had been defiled by rebellion and sin, yet the hope (expressed through the prophets) was that one day, at God's appointed time, God would renew his sovereignty over all things. This longed-for occasion became known as 'the day of the Lord'.

Look at Isaiah 2:6–22, for example, where the prophet describes how God will humble those who have become arrogant and put their trust in the power of idols, wealth and possessions. Verse 11 states, 'The eyes of the arrogant will be humbled and human pride brought low; the Lord alone will be exalted in that day.'

The longing for this wonderful day (see also Isaiah 28:5–6; Hosea 2:16–20; Joel 2:28–32; Zechariah 3:10) was woven into the nation's hopes and dreams over many centuries of exile, return and occupation. The 'day of the Lord' and the 'kingdom of God' became identified with the reign of God's Messiah long before Jesus was born in Bethlehem. Turn again to Isaiah, to that stirring passage read at Christmas carol services: 'And he will be called Wonderful Counsellor, Mighty God, Everlasting Father, Prince of Peace. Of the increase of his government and peace there will be no end. He will reign on David's throne and over his kingdom, establishing and upholding it with justice and righteousness from that time on and for ever' (Isaiah 9:6–7).

As time passed and the memories of the glory days of the kingdom of Israel grew ever more remote, the hope for God's Messiah developed into a focus on gaining political power to overthrow the nation's oppressors. The Messiah would lead them with power and glory to victory. They would then live in a state of renewed paradise, which would last for ever and ever, amen. As the nation's longing developed and intensified, so people began to lose sight of God's greater purposes and project their own manifesto on to the coming Messiah.

That provides the context for the launch of Jesus' ministry (Mark 1:14–15). Jesus went into Galilee, proclaiming the good news of God. 'The time [the day of the Lord] has come,' he said. 'The kingdom of God is near.' No wonder the crowds flocked to Jesus, but we can also understand why the Pharisees and religious leaders were so aghast at his preaching. A carpenter turned preacher, from Nazareth? A man who taught, 'Blessed are the poor, the meek, the persecuted and the peacemakers' (see Matthew 5:1–12)? A man who flouted the sacred laws of Moses? How dare he claim to describe the 'kingdom of God'?

What about us? How do we imagine 'the kingdom of God'? How would we answer Jesus if he sat with us now and asked, 'What is the kingdom of God like?'

Would we think of it as a future state, as we might imagine 'heaven' as some kind of numinous state of perfection with God when the life we know is over? Or could we visualize the beauty of God's reign from the tiny flames of selfless love that we have experienced in ordinary people? How different is God's kingdom from our material world?

You may like to try out this game with some friends. The first person says, 'In my perfect world, everyone would be kind to animals.' The next player responds, 'In my perfect world, everyone would be kind to animals and old people.' The third says, 'In my perfect world, everyone would be kind to animals and old people and no one would be hungry' and so it goes on, as long as people can think of ways to better the world—and we all think we know how to put the world right! This is not just a flippant game; it is a useful way of itemizing how much we feel is wrong with the wonderful world that God created.

So what must God's perspective be? If we look at how Jesus described the kingdom of God, we see that the coming and the spreading of this kingdom is not our initiative but God's. There is no dazzling explosion of power but the silent growth of ordinary small things, like a mustard seed or yeast. It takes time for a seed to become a tree but the tree becomes a haven for other creatures, a complete eco-system (v. 19). We humans enjoy high-visibility deeds, which can be evaluated and praised, but Jesus spoke of the work of the yeast (v. 21). Once mixed with the dough, it cannot be separated or distinguished from the other ingredients within the mixture, yet its effect is dramatic, even essential for the bread to rise.

This is still hard teaching for us to accept. We don't want to wait, to watch and pray. We want to see the world's wrongs put right immediately—the hungry fed, the eyes of the blind opened, swords beaten into ploughshares, all these evocative biblical ideals miraculously taking place at once. Jesus tried to teach his disciples the importance of patience, perseverance and total reliance upon God but, even after his crucifixion and resurrection, they still managed to cling on to old ideas of the kingdom: 'Lord, are you at this time going to restore the kingdom to Israel?' (Acts 1:6).

They did not understand that the kingdom of God could be attained only by personal and individual renewal of heart and attitude, and the words of Jesus retain their age-old challenge to each one of us now, today.

The media are full, these days, of stories about human rights, trade justice and global interdependence, but what good are human rights without the human responsibilities enshrined by Jesus' teaching of God's kingdom? Mark may have written in his Gospel that Jesus taught the 'good news' of God (1:15), but Jesus also taught of judgment and consequence for those who wilfully make a choice against God. It is not all good news: we cannot pick and choose the bits of the Bible that suit us and leave out the uncomfortable parts.

Jesus said, 'When the Son of Man comes in his glory… all the nations will be gathered before him, and he will separate the people one from another as a shepherd separates the sheep from the goats' (Matthew 25:31–32). 'Judgment' is not a popular word in our culture: we like to roll out the peace and understanding but go easy on the judgment side. In doing this, we all make the same serious mistake: we underestimate the power of evil in our midst and we underestimate the almighty power of the living God to bring his kingdom into our hearts, our communities and our world.

God's kingdom is where ordinary, faithful people live to serve him, echoing the worship songs of the psalmists, the prophets, Zechariah and Mary, the mother of Jesus. Let's thank God for the glimpses we already see, and pray for the courage to nurture the 'seeds' and the 'yeast' of the kingdom when we discover them working in our lives.

For reflection

'The kingdom of God does not come with your careful observation, nor will people say, "Here it is," or "There it is," because the kingdom of God is within you.'

LUKE 17:20–21

Prayer

Lord, help me to seek your justice and mercy by my words and actions, so that your kingdom may truly live in me.

Chapter 15

'Why did you doubt?'

After [Jesus] had dismissed [the disciples], he went up on a mountainside by himself to pray. When evening came, he was there alone, but the boat was already a considerable distance from land, buffeted by the waves because the wind was against it. During the fourth watch of the night Jesus went out to them, walking on the lake. When the disciples saw him walking on the lake, they were terrified, 'It's a ghost,' they said, and cried out in fear. But Jesus immediately said to them, 'Take courage! It is I. Don't be afraid.' 'Lord, if it's you,' Peter replied, 'tell me to come to you on the water.' 'Come,' he said. Then Peter got down out of the boat, walked on the water and came toward Jesus. But when he saw the wind, he was afraid and, beginning to sink, cried out, 'Lord, save me!' Immediately Jesus reached out his hand and caught him. 'You of little faith,' he said, 'why did you doubt?' And when they climbed into the boat, the wind died down. Then those who were in the boat worshipped him, saying, 'Truly you are the Son of God.'
MATTHEW 14:23–33

This 14th chapter of Matthew is a blockbuster. It has only 36 verses, but what vivid insight into the life of the disciples! They are propelled on an emotional rollercoaster from the depths of sadness at John the Baptist's murder to the heights of exhilaration as thousands sit down to eat together. No sooner have they experienced this miracle than they find themselves alone on the Sea of Galilee, storm-tossed and terrified. Then, from the pit of danger they are lifted to the mysteries of worship and the reality of God's presence.

As Matthew hurtles from one breathtaking revelation to the next, we find ourselves entering upon our own journey of discovery.

When we think of 'the disciples', we may immediately register who comprised this group, but do we ever stop to think how little we know about any of them? Just a few snippets tell us who were fishermen, who was the tax collector, Zealot and so on, but we have no other personal details except for their names and the fact that Peter had a wife and mother-in-law.

As a result, we tend to create our own stylized impressions of these men. For instance, who was the doubting disciple? Hands shoot up to incriminate Thomas, whose one recorded doubt about the authenticity of the resurrection has branded him for all time (John 20:25). In these verses from Matthew, however, it is not Thomas but Peter who begins to sink because of insistent, niggling doubt. We never describe him as 'doubting Peter' but, if we piece together strands from across the Gospels, it becomes clear that at different times, all the disciples had misgivings and second thoughts (John 1:46; Luke 8:25; Mark 9:32; 14:50). These were not haloed saints but working Galilean men (Acts 4:13), who worshipped their master but could nevertheless be wracked with doubt.

Is there anybody in the world who can truthfully claim that they have never had any doubts at all? For me, one of the most encouraging characteristics of the disciples is the way in which they seem to share the same uncertainties that we know today. We should also bear in mind that the Gospel authors wrote what they did with the benefit of hindsight. In retrospect, they could see God's great plan and purpose unfolding, and words from their scriptures took on new meaning because of what Jesus had said and done. Most of us will have similar experiences, in which events make sense only when we look back and realize that, despite our fears, God's presence has never failed.

In Matthew's account of that terrifying night on the lake, we read that the disciples had been instructed by Jesus to go to the other side of the lake without him (v. 22). Out in the fishing boat, in the dark, heaving about in the wind and the rain, the experienced fishermen among them would still have been fairly confident, in familiar territory, but what reduced them to absolute terror was the unexpected sight of someone walking on the water towards them. This really spooked them—it wasn't humanly possible!

Once again, Jesus spoke words that God had spoken through Moses and the prophets: 'Don't be afraid.' At the sound of Jesus' voice, Peter's courage returned and his impulsive nature took over. He couldn't wait to reach his master—until, that is, he got out of the boat. Suddenly, disbelief at what he was doing gave way to panic. He faltered, out of his depth and sinking—literally about to drown in his doubt.

Peter had jumped out of the boat trusting in his own strength to reach Jesus but, when his own physical and spiritual strength failed him, Jesus reached out in love to save him. Then Jesus asked him, 'Why did you doubt?' (v. 31). I wonder, was the emphasis on 'why' or on 'you'?

Let's take the 'why' first: '*Why* did you doubt?' We can think about all the miracles Peter had witnessed and the life-transforming teaching he had heard. Jesus was his beloved master; surely he had lived alongside him long enough to know in his heart that Jesus would never fail him? Why couldn't he trust? What more did he need to know about his Lord? Was Jesus inviting Peter to ask himself a deeper question than he wanted to answer?

Then again, the emphasis may have been on 'you': 'Why did *you* doubt?' Peter could have been the senior disciple in terms of his age; he was definitely within the selected inner group of the disciples, along with James and John (see Luke 8:51; Matthew 26:37). Jesus stayed at Peter's house in Capernaum (Mark 1:29), and Mark places his name first when recording the transfiguration: 'Jesus took Peter, James and John with him…' (9:2). There were high expectations of Peter, and Jesus would say to him shortly after this experience; 'I tell you that you are Peter, and on this rock I will build my church, and the gates of Hades will not overcome it' (Matthew 16:18). The other men looked to Peter for leadership because of all his enthusiasm and faith, but now, to their surprise, the fisherman disciple from Capernaum mirrored their own uncertainties.

I believe we need to take encouragement from Peter's actions. He was a warm, impulsive, always down-to-earth character, brimming with good intentions but also enduring some very public humiliation. Peter wanted to be first to meet Jesus on the water, but within seconds he was floundering; Peter declared he would die for Jesus (Matthew 26:35), but within hours he denied even knowing him (vv. 69–75). Peter cut off the ear of the high priest's servant in the garden of Gethsemane, but this same man fled in fear with all the others, leaving Jesus alone (v. 56b). This was a man of passion, faith, loyalty and courage, but, like all of us, vulnerable to doubts and temptations. He displayed all the highs and lows of our humanity, and through it all Jesus loved him and forgave him. Despite Peter's volatile character, Jesus knew that he would become the 'rock' for early believers and, in the power of the Holy Spirit, it was Peter who stood up in Jerusalem to declare Jesus Christ's Lordship fearlessly to all the world (Acts 2:14).

I wonder if I can bear the gaze of Jesus as he asks me, 'Why did you doubt?' I know he understands my good intentions and my heart's desires; he forgives my negative attitudes and heals my shame. Why is it that, even in the light and glory of God's love for me in Jesus, there are still times when the shadowy fingers of doubt threaten to unhinge my tender faith?

All through my life, when words and thoughts have failed me, I have found strength and inspiration in the poetry of hymns and songs. I would like to share with you some words by the Swiss pastor Edmond L. Budry (1854–1932), which make a wonderful prayer of rededication when our faith has wavered.

No more we doubt Thee, glorious Prince of Life;
Life is naught without Thee: aid us in our strife;
Make us more than conquerors, through Thy deathless love:
Bring us safe through Jordan to Thy home above:

Thine be the glory, risen, conquering Son,
Endless is the victory Thou o'er death hast won.

When we pray with the conviction of the saints who have gone before us and become aware of the uniting bond of prayer from Christians around the world, we will discover that our own faith is strengthened. Life will always throw biting winds and surging waves at us, to buffet and submerge us, but in every storm we are held by a greater power than our own. We cannot save ourselves. Peter found this out by bitter trial and error, over a lifetime, and I suppose that sometimes it is only by bitter experience that we learn to lean on our Lord. Be wary of the person who claims a never-wavering, incessantly upbeat faith!

For reflection

Ponder these words from a letter written by Peter to encourage new believers.

To those who through the righteousness of our God and Saviour Jesus Christ have received a faith as precious as ours… We did not follow cleverly invented stories when we told you about the power and coming of our Lord Jesus Christ, but we were eyewitnesses of his majesty… Grow in the grace and knowledge of our Lord and Saviour Jesus Christ. To him be glory both now and for ever! Amen.
2 PETER 1:1, 16; 3:18

Chapter 16

'Whose portrait is this?'

Later [the chief priests, teachers of the Law and elders] sent some of the Pharisees and Herodians to Jesus to catch him in his words. They came to him and said, 'Teacher, we know you are a man of integrity. You aren't swayed by others, because you pay no attention to who they are; but you teach the way of God in accordance with the truth. Is it right to pay taxes to Caesar or not? Should we pay or shouldn't we?' But Jesus knew their hypocrisy. 'Why are you trying to trap me?' he asked. 'Bring me a denarius and let me look at it.' They brought the coin, and he asked them, 'Whose portrait is this? And whose inscription?' 'Caesar's,' they replied. Then Jesus said to them, 'Give to Caesar what is Caesar's and to God what is God's.' And they were amazed at him.

MARK 12:13–17

Tax! Just the mention of the word sends blood pressures through the roof. We unite in hissing resentment against being taxed, even though we benefit from the use of taxes. Although we may agree that taxation of some sort is essential to run public services, people never agree on the fairness of the tax they have to pay. Thus it was, and ever more shall be, but the first-century Jews had more reason than we do to be bitter over taxes.

Taxation is one of a number of legacies that the Romans have left us, along with paved roads, sanitation, central heating and the population census. In the eyes of every first-century Jew, however, the 'foreign' tax system was a loathsome symbol of occupation. They saw little return for their taxes but were sharply aware that the money was being squandered on pagan temples and luxurious living for the ruling élite. The payment of their taxes underpinned and ensured the continuation of their oppression by the Romans. It was a bitter problem.

The tax system had three tiers: ground tax, income tax and poll tax. The poll tax was levied on all men aged between 14 and 65 and women aged 12 to 65. Ground tax was a tax on one-tenth of all grain and one-fifth of all fruit and wine, and this tax could be paid either in kind or in money. Then there was income tax, which worked out at approximately one per cent of a man's earnings. Joseph would have paid income tax at his carpenter's shop in Nazareth, and both he and Mary would have paid the poll tax. Jesus, too, from the age of 14, would have been liable to pay tax. Somehow it's strange to think of Jesus as a tax payer!

Not all the Jews were compliant with the Roman government, though. There was a small group of insurgents, the Zealots, who agitated in and around Galilee and Judea in Jesus' time, and among them one—Judas the Gaulonite—was notorious. He attacked the Roman system vociferously: 'Taxation is no better than an introduction to slavery!' Another slogan was 'No tribute to the Romans.'

Since the question of taxes was such a raw subject, Jewish tax collectors were despised and shunned for their perceived collaboration with 'the enemy'. It's interesting, then, to find both a tax collector (Matthew) and a Zealot (Simon) among Jesus' inner circle of twelve disciples (see Matthew 10:2–4).

If you look back at Mark 11, you will find the context for our passage. Jesus had already stumped the chief priests, teachers of the law and the elders, who had done their best to trick him into committing blasphemy (vv. 27–33). In answer to their question, he had brilliantly returned another to them: 'John's baptism—was it from heaven, or from men?' (v. 30). These learned men could not answer Jesus satisfactorily, which made them look foolish. Jesus then went on to tell the parable of the tenants (12:1–11), an obvious reference to their rejection of his authority. They wanted to arrest him but were afraid to make any public move against him because of his obvious popularity with all the people (v. 12). Masking their venom, they melted away—but not for long.

Imagine the chief priests summoning the teachers of the Law and the elders into a private room. Spitting with rage and indignation, they scheme and plot their next assault. They select 'some of the Pharisees and Herodians' (v. 13) to set the next trap. I wonder who came up with the brilliant idea to corner Jesus with a tax question. It was the perfect approach, for whether Jesus answered 'yes' or 'no' it would be the wrong answer. If he said 'Yes', that it was right to pay taxes to Caesar, the crowds could be easily manoeuvred into thinking him a traitor to his countrymen, thereby losing him his following and his credibility. If he said 'No', that it wasn't right to pay Caesar the taxes, then they could hand him over to the authorities for treason against Rome. In the minds of those religious leaders, they had Jesus beaten, game, set and match.

Mark is not alone in recounting this potentially disastrous encounter. The account is repeated almost word for word in Matthew 22:15–22 and Luke 20:20–26.

Herodians and Pharisees were not the closest of friends—in fact, they were at opposite ends of the spectrum of ritual piety—and this bizarre temporary alliance shows how desperate the temple leaders were to undermine the ministry of Jesus of Nazareth. Jesus saw right through these men, however. He was not fooled by hypocrites sent to trap him.

Hidden within this story, we even catch a glimpse of the way Jesus and his disciples arranged their 'housekeeping'. Jesus had to ask for a coin because he himself did not carry a purse. That was Judas Iscariot's job, one given to a highly trusted individual. With hindsight, the fact that Judas was the group's treasurer sheds a warmer light on the man's integrity, although John, with the hindsight of the betrayal and Judas' subsequent suicide, leaves us his jaundiced view of the man: 'He was a thief; as keeper of the money bag, he used to help himself to what was put into it' (John 12:6).

But back to our story. Jesus asks for a denarius, a coin that was the equivalent of a day's wage. (Maybe Judas only had small change and Jesus had to ask the Pharisees and Herodians to bring him the coin.) When they produce the coin, he takes the sting from their question immediately by asking his own: 'Whose portrait is this?' (v. 16).

The currency of the Roman world bore the image of the emperor, with deep implications in the minds of both Jews and Romans. To the Roman, the emperor was the high priest of the nation, and this designation was inscribed on the reverse of the coin. As a conquering power, they were able to impose their coinage on the defeated country, and this gave them an enormous sense of superiority and power. The coins 'belonged' to the emperor and it was his mercy that allowed them to be used.

To the Jewish mind, however, there was no high priest except their own, and Caesar's claim was blasphemous. Caesar was a Gentile and a licentious brute, whose army was loathed for its presence in the land and its brutal repression of the people. Being forced to use a coin with Caesar's head on it was a daily reminder of their subservience to a foreign power. With these contrasting thoughts running through the heads of the Pharisees, Herodians, disciples and supporting crowd, Jesus delivers his razor-sharp response: 'Give to Caesar what is Caesar's and to God what is God's' (v. 17).

In a dozen words, Jesus made a declaration for loyalty to civilian power while at the same time alluding to the greater power of Almighty God, to whom the people had a duty of obedience and loyalty. It was an exemplary answer, which silenced the critics and sent them back to the high priests, teachers of the Law, Sadducees and elders to hatch an even more determined plot against Jesus (see Matthew 26:3–5).

Jesus had made it plain that the people had a responsibility to uphold their rulers, however much that hurt them. He also reminded his hearers that they had obligations and duties towards God, the king of the universe, who had given each one of them the gift of life. His words were almost proverbial in their brevity and eternal relevance.

Like our Roman and Jewish forebears, we have coins depicting the monarch's head, a symbol of national pride and allegiance. We also have credit and debit cards bearing a variety of other names and logos, each of which puts us under obligation to repay. If we imagine Jesus asking us the question 'Whose portrait is this?' I believe it is a challenge to look at how we have placed our own personal obligations. Are there occasions when we are so busy making our repayments to banks and department stores that we lose sight of our obligation to our God? Have we been too occupied with material loyalty cards, so that we have misplaced our loyalty to God? In this story, Jesus didn't tell us to put one before the other but rather to make sure we get the balance right.

As Paul wrote to the first Corinthian Christians, 'Each of you should give what you have decided in your heart to give, not reluctantly or under compulsion, for God loves a cheerful giver' (2 Corinthians 9:7). I don't think this was a tongue-in-cheek quip, more a nudge to the understanding that the last thing to be converted when we come to faith will be our purses and wallets.

It's interesting that, two thousand years later, those of us living in a prevailing climate of monetary debt can still find Jesus' words on money so relevant. Remember the parable of the men who fell into debt, as recorded in Matthew 18:23–35, and the transformation of Zacchaeus in Luke 19:8. Churches today have a huge responsibility to teach good stewardship of all resources, including our money. As we take a cool, objective look at whose portrait we put first in our lives, let us also hear the words of Jesus: 'You cannot serve both God and Money' (Luke 16:13). The choice is ours.

In our dealings over money and with other people, we are the 'face' of Christianity: we represent our Lord to the world. That's a truly awesome responsibility, and we will probably fail in it many more times than we succeed, but it is a responsibility that we share with millions of our Christian brothers and sisters worldwide and one in which we will be strengthened and encouraged by the power of the Holy Spirit.

Parents have always lavished as much as they can afford when it comes to their childrens' birthdays, holidays or Christmas. Their generosity is born out of love: it's not a chore, nor do they begrudge going without things for themselves. Such is the response of love. Let us take a look at how we respond to God through his Son Jesus. Could we become 'cheerful givers' for the sake of the one who gave his life for us, to pay the price of your sin and mine (1 Corinthians 7:23)?

Prayer

Lord, help me to make the right decisions about money today. May my principles be set by your standards of love, forgiveness, justice and mercy, so that my way of life and giving will display the 'face' of Christ.

Chapter 17

'Are you asleep?'

They went to a place called Gethsemane, and Jesus said to his disciples, 'Sit here while I pray.' He took Peter, James and John along with him, and he began to be deeply distressed and troubled. 'My soul is overwhelmed with sorrow to the point of death,' he said to them. 'Stay here and keep watch.' Going a little farther, he fell to the ground and prayed that if possible the hour might pass from him. 'Abba, Father,' he said, everything is possible for you. Take this cup from me. Yet not what I will, but what you will.' Then he returned to his disciples and found them sleeping. 'Simon,' he said to Peter, 'are you asleep? Could you not keep watch for one hour? Watch and pray so that you will not fall into temptation. The spirit is willing, but the body is weak.'

MARK 14:32–38

Have you ever fallen asleep when you meant to stay awake?

It's not a great surprise that the disciples were tired. Since their walk up from Galilee to the holy city of Jerusalem for Passover, the days had been exceptionally busy. Probably none of them slept very well the night after Jesus had ridden into the city with the crowds shouting, 'Hosanna! Blessed is he who comes in the name of the Lord!' (Mark 11:9). What a reception! Their hearts were racing with anticipation about what would happen next.

Then, when Jesus enraged the temple leaders by overturning the moneychanging tables (11:15–17), the disciples were probably kept awake later, worrying. Was their master deliberately antagonizing the chief priests and teachers of the law? It was all getting too dangerous in the city for these men of Galilee.

Perhaps, for a couple of days, they kept a low profile, staying over in Bethany with Mary, Martha and Lazarus. Even so, Jesus had crammed their minds with teaching that they didn't understand. He talked of leaving them, of suffering, of giving them a Comforter (John 14:16, 26, KJV). He told them not to be afraid, but to trust him (John 14:1, 27). They just couldn't take it all in.

After their Passover meal together and the walk out of the city up into the soft darkness of the Gethsemane olive groves, the disciples were shattered. They slumped against the stocky olive trunks and were asleep in moments.

I've heard preachers denouncing the disciples for failing to watch with their Lord for one short hour. Surely, though, this is an unhelpful and negative response to an understandably human reaction. None of us can be certain what we would have done had we been there in Gethsemane. After such a varied and packed week, I expect I may have been among the first to shut my eyes. There would have been a sense of peace and security among the sheltering trees, with the noise and danger of the city left behind, across the Kidron valley. The disciples would have thought they could relax at last.

That leaves us with an intriguing question. If Peter and the brothers James and John were asleep, who was listening to Jesus' most intimate and agonizing prayers?

Some have suggested that Jesus repeated to his disciples what he had said in his prayers but, in the highly charged atmosphere of fear and emotion that followed, with the lanterns of Judas and the hostile crowd moving ever closer, that scenario is hardly likely. My guess is that the eavesdropper was probably John Mark, the young man who had followed the disciples from the upper room and fled from Gethsemane when Jesus was arrested (see Mark 14:51–52).

This is the Mark who, some three decades later, collated the first Gospel with the first-hand recollections of the disciple Peter. Just think how Jesus' abject agony would have burned into young Mark's heart! The man whom he hero-worshipped from the fringe of events, the rabbi whose words confounded Pharisees and Sadducees and whose miraculous touch gave healing and hope to the sick, the Jesus who should be 'King of the Jews', lying prostrate on the ground, tormented and distraught—no one could forget that sight.

Nowhere else in the Gospels is the humanity of Jesus more clearly drawn than in this episode. It is such a private anguish that the mere reading of the verses is almost embarrassing, for most of us feel helpless in the face of someone else's agony. Nevertheless, Jesus wanted and needed his closest followers with him on that dark night. We can understand that, also, from our own experiences. Situations may not improve but they are made more bearable if someone is alongside us.

These verses record a glimpse into Jesus' isolation, the terrible loneliness into which his friends could not enter. They didn't understand their master's urgent need for them to 'keep watch' (v. 34). It's something for us all to ponder: when we reach the limit of our human endurance, we are outside the understanding even of those closest to us. We are alone with God. For many people, this is quite a frightening place to be. Catapulted out of our comfort zone, stripped of confidence and identity, we too can find ourselves overwhelmed with sorrow. Jesus cried out to his God, his Father, his rock and his redeemer, and we find the essence of his prayer echoed in what we call the Lord's Prayer: 'Thy will be done' (Matthew 6:10).

Jesus did not put himself first but accepted God's will for his life and death. We can take on board these words of Jesus, 'Not my will, but yours be done' (Luke 22:42), in which he subjugated his own desires to the will of his Father and God. Through the guidance of the Holy Spirit, we can make them our own prayer, to strengthen us for whatever daunts and challenges us.

Jesus left his prayer to go back to Peter, James and John, and found that they were sleeping, although he had told them to keep watch, to be alert to any needs from the group and on guard for imminent dangers. What does his question to them mean for us:

'Are you asleep?' Why should it matter if we are asleep?

Have you noticed the number of times the phrases 'keep watch' or 'wake up' are used in the Bible? Look at Isaiah 51:17, Psalm 141:3 and Revelation 3:2, for example.

Jesus had emphasized the need to be watchful and on guard when he told the parable of the five wise and five foolish virgins (Matthew 25:1–13). The foolish virgins were no less enthusiastic about waiting for the bridegroom but they were not adequately prepared for the long wait. By contrast, the wise young women had reserves on which to draw. Christians need not only to be alert and prepared for the Lord to come at any time, but also to be aware of the work that God wants us to do in our individual situations. While we wait for Jesus' final return in glory, he calls us to watch and pray over what goes on in our world, to demonstrate a different code of conduct, to be the flavoursome salt in the stew of life (Matthew 5:13).

In our prosperous Western society, it is very convenient to close our eyes to a multitude of situations when perhaps we should be asking ourselves whether Jesus would have us be watchful. Does Jesus find us asleep to the gratuitous violence of computer and video games offered to children in the name of entertainment? Does he find our eyes closed to the exploitation of women and girls trafficked across continents and held in modern-day slavery? Does Jesus sigh as we doze through the startling statistical rises in sexual diseases, drug, alcohol and gambling addictions and domestic violence? We must not 'sleep' when there is much valuable work to do. We may be full of good intentions but, as Jesus knows, 'the spirit is willing, but the body is weak' (Mark 14:38).

The apostle Paul wrote, 'So then, let us not be like others, who are asleep, but let us be alert and self-controlled' (1 Thessalonians 5:6). In the series of letters to the churches in the book of Revelation, we also read, 'Wake up! Strengthen what remains and is about to die' (3:2).

The book of Revelation was written at a time when Christians were experiencing fierce opposition and persecution. Perversely, there is nothing like opposition to shake us into stronger faith and more active service. Look at the astonishing growth of Christianity in China, a country whose government viciously clamped down on religion in the last century. We can no longer 'sleepwalk' as disciples when faith becomes a matter of life and death, here and now.

Let's make sure we are fully ready and awake when our Lord Jesus returns. The only preparation we can make is to submit our will to his, to say each day, 'Your will be done.'

Prayer

Lord, I pray for the self-discipline to tune my heart and mind to the opportunities that you open for me. Show me ways in which I can serve my Saviour in the needs of those with whom I live, work or relax. Rouse me from my self-centredness to seek your will in all things.

Chapter 18

'My God, my God, why...?'

At the sixth hour darkness came over the whole land until the ninth hour. And at the ninth hour Jesus cried out in a loud voice, '*Eloi, Eloi, lama sabachthani?*'—which means, 'My God, my God, why have you forsaken me?' When some of those standing near heard this, they said, 'Listen, he's calling Elijah.' One man ran, filled a sponge with wine vinegar, put it on a stick, and offered it to Jesus to drink. 'Now leave him alone. Let's see if Elijah comes to take him down,' he said. With a loud cry, Jesus breathed his last. The curtain of the temple was torn in two from top to bottom. And when the centurion, who stood there in front of Jesus, heard his cry and saw how he died, he said, 'Surely this man was the Son of God!' Some women were watching from a distance. Among them were Mary Magdalene, Mary the mother of James the younger and of Joses, and Salome. In Galilee these women had followed him and cared for his needs. Many other women who had come up with him to Jerusalem were also there.

MARK 15:33–41

If there is one word that resonates with every despairing heart, it is the desolate cry, 'Why?' From the parents whose child is killed in a road accident to the wife whose husband goes off with another woman, from the victim of horrendous warfare to the person struck by incurable illness, that same small word is uttered. 'Why?'

Surely it was the sob of Mary as she watched her beloved son being nailed to the cross by rough Roman soldiers, and the silent cry of the women who tried to comfort her. I doubt if there is anyone alive who hasn't, at some time or other, asked God, 'Why?'

These words that Jesus spoke from the cross have become well-known, and great theological debates have been held over the exact moment of Jesus' separation from God as he carried the sins of the world. His isolation was complete. In the words of the prophet Isaiah, 'He was oppressed and afflicted... he was led like a lamb to the slaughter... For he was cut off from the land of the living; for the transgression of my people he was stricken' (53:7–8).

All four Gospels record in varying detail the dreadful death of our Lord Jesus Christ. Both Mark 15:34 and Matthew 27:46 record that Jesus cried out, 'My God, my God, why have you forsaken me?' while Luke and John include other words (see Luke 23:43–46; John 19:26–30). From the four accounts, and from remarkably few verses, we are able to build a full picture of those horrendous hours. I believe that as we unpack each fragment of the hours leading to Jesus' death, we will discover far deeper meaning from Mark's succinct report than a straight reading imparts.

One of the saddest moments for Jesus had already taken place: 'Then everyone deserted him and fled' (Mark 14:50). His disciples had disappeared into the night, frightened for their lives. Jesus had been marched off to the high priest to face interrogation alone; he had been dragged bleeding and stumbling through the narrow streets of Jerusalem, so bereft of help that the soldiers had needed to commandeer a stranger, Simon of Cyrene, to carry the cross. Beaten, hit in the face, spat at, insulted and jeered, finally he was stripped naked and nailed into position, waiting to die.

Mark is very specific about the time when Jesus was nailed on the cross: 'It was the third hour' (15:25), or nine o'clock in the morning. Jesus hung for three excruciating hours, with his mother Mary and the other women watching and waiting as close to his wracked body as they were allowed. There were others watching, too—passers-by, first-century rubbernecks gawping at the torture, and the curious bystanders who wondered whether Jesus would perform his last and greatest miracle and come down from the cross. It seems that even the chief priests and teachers of the law were standing by, mocking him, along with those crucified with him (v. 32).

This was the darkest time of Jesus' life. Mark tells us that he had been offered 'wine mixed with myrrh', which he refused (v. 23): it was something that the women of Jerusalem did for those being crucified, giving the drink that could dull the victim's pain as an act of charity. John's Gospel tells us that Jesus did take a drink of wine vinegar later (John 19:28–30).

Psalm 69 holds verses that would have been familiar to Jesus and his disciples, verses whose terrible prophetic accuracy would have made his followers tremble: 'Scorn has broken my heart and has left me helpless; I looked for sympathy, but there was none, for comforters, but I found none. They put gall in my food and gave me vinegar for my thirst' (vv. 19–21). Yet when Jesus cried out, 'My God, my God, why have you forsaken me?' it was not this psalm that he was quoting, but Psalm 22. Psalm 69 pulses with the desire for vengeance, whereas Jesus asked God's forgiveness on those who tormented him: 'Father, forgive them, for they do not know what they are doing' (Luke 23:34).

Mark writes that 'darkness came over the whole land' at noon (15:33). Here is the divine paradox that Jesus, the light of the world, hung in the darkness of human cruelty—but we can read these words with the knowledge of the resurrection and the promise found in the opening lines of John's Gospel: 'The light shines in the darkness, and the darkness did not overcome it' (John 1:5, NRSV). There is hope, a new dawn after the longest of nights.

In the midst of his suffering, from the depths of his soul, Jesus cried out—not a cry to his 'Abba' Father, but in the words of the psalmist, 'My God, my God, why have you forsaken me?' Did Jesus really feel that God had left him?

I think we need to pause and read the whole of Psalm 22 to discover its intention and also to see that this particular sentence can be taken two ways. The early Greek manuscripts did not use punctuation (and ancient Hebrew used neither vowels nor punctuation), so it could be read either as 'My God, my God, why have you forsaken me?' or as 'My God, my God, why? Have you forsaken me?'

The beginning of this psalm is definitely a suffering lament, but what an ending it turns out to have! It is actually a psalm of thanksgiving and triumph, concluding with the amazing lines, 'Future generations will be told about the Lord. They will proclaim his righteousness to a people yet unborn—for he has done it' (vv. 30–31). John's Gospel confirms this picture of an ultimate triumph: 'When he had received the drink, Jesus said, "It is finished." With that, he bowed his head and gave up his spirit' (19:30).

This leaves us with an enigma. If some of the last words Jesus spoke before dying came from a psalm of thanksgiving and included the statement, 'It is finished' (meaning 'accomplished, completed, paid in full'), how are we to understand his question, 'Why have you forsaken me?'

To try to glimpse an answer, we need to juxtapose the full humanity of Jesus with his full divinity. We are dealing here with concepts beyond our limited capacity to understand fully, as Paul noted when he wrote about seeing 'but a poor reflection' (1 Corinthians 13:12), or, as the King James Bible puts it, 'through a glass, darkly'. Mark's graphic description of the dying Jesus is heightened by the quotation from Psalm 22, confronting us with the depths of agony and isolation that Jesus endured. In those moments of his human dying, he sensed God's rejection of the world's sin. He was appalled by even a momentary separation from his Father. In human terms we may ask, did his trust in his God and Father waver? If it did, then there is consolation for us as we battle, from time to time, with our own wobbling and wavering faith.

The humanity of Jesus in this moment makes an immediate connection with everyone who has ever cried out, who has ever asked 'the world's eternal "why?"' There is indeed solidarity in suffering. We have a Saviour who understands what it is like to be isolated, to despair, to feel the full weight of tragedy and pain. We have a Saviour who understands us.

Just think how the disciples must have felt on that Holy Saturday, terrified, despairing and alone. How could God have allowed their beloved master to be crucified? Why? Did they rail against God for abandoning them?

As the groups of early Christian believers and their leaders suffered persecution and martyrdom, there must have been many agonizing moments when they felt that God had forsaken them, too. The first recorded martyr was Stephen, stoned to death outside one of the city gates of Jerusalem (Acts 7:58–60). This must have been a shattering blow for members of the early Church and a severe test of their faith. In the following years, James (the brother of John) was put to death by the sword (Acts 12:2) and tradition says that Peter was crucified upside down. Throughout history, Christian saints have been persecuted and martyred, each death causing people to cry out 'Why?' and feel forsaken in their grief.

The words of Paul speak directly to such situations: 'Who shall separate us from the love of Christ? Shall trouble or hardship or persecution or famine or nakedness or danger or sword? … No, in all these things we are more than conquerors through him who loved us' (Romans 8:35, 37).

Are there times when you yourself feel forsaken by God? Times when you can't understand what is happening in your life or the life of someone you love? Times when you stare at a situation and all you can murmur is, 'My God, my God, why…?'

We may never find the answer to our question in this life, but it is in the thrashing and writhing, the praying and searching that we reach out to Jesus—and he becomes our answer.

Prayer

Lord, I know that the sun shines above the darkest clouds. Help me to remember that even when I cannot feel you near me, you are still with me. Help me to remember always that nothing can separate me from your love and care.

Chapter 19

'Why are you crying?'

'Woman,' he said, 'why are you crying? Who is it you are looking for?' Thinking he was the gardener, she said, 'Sir, if you have carried him away, tell me where you have put him, and I will get him.' Jesus said to her, 'Mary.' She turned toward him and cried out in Aramaic, 'Rabboni!' (which means Teacher). Jesus said, 'Do not hold on to me, for I have not yet returned to the Father. Go instead to my brothers and tell them, "I am returning to my Father and your Father, to my God and your God."' Mary Magdalene went to the disciples with the news: 'I have seen the Lord!' And she told them that he had said these things to her.
JOHN 20:15–18

In the same way as we might ask a child, 'What's the matter?' Jesus found Mary by the open tomb, alone and weeping, and asked her, 'Why are you crying?'

Just put yourself in Mary's shoes for a moment: she had stood for six hours at Golgotha, 'the Place of the Skull', the horrible place for public crucifixions, overwhelmed with anguish as she and the other women watched their beloved Jesus draw each agonized breath. She had wept at his suffering, sobbed at his death and sat wailing with grief throughout the sabbath, longing for the dark hours to pass so that she could go to his tomb and administer her last acts of tender reverence.

Sleepless and despairing, Mary was wrung out. She must have felt that she couldn't cry any more. Finally, she couldn't wait for dawn any longer and made her way to the tomb 'while it was still dark' (John 20:1). Then, when she reached the garden where

Joseph of Arimathea and the Pharisee Nicodemus had laid Jesus' body, she saw through the gloom that the stone had been rolled away and his body was gone. It was the last straw—the end of everything. Her tears began all over again. What had happened? Surely the precious, broken body of her Lord had not been taken and thrown into the communal pit to rot alongside unclaimed criminals? She needed to grieve over his body, to do all she could for the man who had done so much for her.

When there is no body to mourn, the psychological pain of those who have suffered bereavement can be hard to bear. Consider for a moment the families of those who were drowned in the 2004 tsunami but whose bodies were never found. Remember, too, the hundreds of families robbed of a body to mourn and lay to rest by the terrorist attacks on the Twin Towers and elsewhere. Those were very public tragedies but think also of the private agony for families whose loved ones, children and adults, have simply vanished. In the same way that any one of us might react, Mary just couldn't understand where Jesus' body had gone.

Not knowing what else to do, she ran to where Peter and John were staying (v. 2). From the fact that Mary knew exactly where to find them, we might deduce that they were with their usual friends in Bethany. If it was still dark, she probably woke them to tell them her alarming discovery, relying on Peter and John to know what to do. Breathlessly, she followed them back to the garden. Imagine how she must have felt when, after looking inside the tomb, 'the disciples went back to their homes' (v. 10), as there was nothing else to do except hide from the authorities. Mary was left standing outside the tomb, alone with her own thoughts and feelings.

With swollen eyes and bowed head, she peers into the tomb, and two figures from inside ask her why she is crying (v. 13). All her heartache and misery spill out in her reply: 'They have taken my Lord away, and I don't know where they have put him' (v. 13). It is a statement of despair. Mary then turns away from the tomb to find someone else standing close by: perhaps he knows what has happened. This stranger enquires, 'Woman, why are you crying?' (v. 15).

Why was she crying? Her entire world had come to an end! What else could she do?

Mary was the first witness to the joyous miracle of resurrection but, initially, she could concentrate only on her own personal sorrow—sorrow that Jesus transformed into ecstasy as she heard her name, 'Mary', spoken by the dear familiar voice (v. 16). We often experience tears of joy as well as tears of sorrow, and I'm convinced that Mary's joy would have been expressed in more tears at the sheer glorious astonishment of seeing her Lord alive. As much as we marvel at this unique encounter outside the empty tomb, however, the degree of Mary's joy remains beyond our experience and understanding. That joy is reserved until our own meeting with Jesus in the life that awaits us.

Mary Magdalene was not only the very first witness to the resurrection; she was also the first evangelist. She sped to find the disciples and exclaim those immortal words, 'I have seen the Lord!' (v. 18).

So many tears have been shed in the course of human history—tears of anger, pain, bitterness, shame, sorrow, guilt, frustration, hurt, loneliness. What makes us weep, and how would we answer Jesus if he found us in tears and asked, 'Why are you crying?'

Jenny was often in church, even though her grown-up children had long stopped attending. She was neither shy nor extravert, a faithful worshipper who preferred to stay on the fringe. One Sunday, the minister's text was taken from Ephesians 1:5, a verse about adoption. In his illustration he spoke about the effect his own adoption had had upon his life.

From the front, the minister could see Jenny becoming more and more distressed. She ended up in floods of tears. After the service, in the confidential setting of the counselling room, Jenny revealed what had broken down her defences.

Back in the 'swinging 60s', Jenny found she was pregnant—aged 15. Her father was incandescent and her parents made arrangements for the baby to be adopted. Jenny had no say in the matter. She lurched through her pregnancy, cowed by shame and anxiety, and she saw her baby girl for just a few hours.

Thirty-five years later, she still cried for the daughter she was forced to give away, the life she wondered about every single day. She cried because she worried about what had become of the little girl, now probably a mother herself. She cried from shame and from guilt and from a fear that her daughter might have grown up feeling that her mother hadn't loved her. It was usually a secret, silent weeping that her husband, family and friends never saw.

Over time, Jenny began to gain the confidence to believe that she could give all that hidden pain to God in Jesus. In prayer she developed a cathartic release of the tensions that had gripped and stifled her, emotionally and spiritually, over all those years. Of course, nothing could fill the loss of her first child but she was able to lose the guilt and shame and accept her own adoption by God. Gradually she found the peace that had so long alluded her. At last, her tears ceased.

Jesus himself wept on at least two recorded occasions. He wept for the plight of Jerusalem, for its leaders' obduracy and blindness (Luke 19:41) and he wept when Lazarus died (John 11:35). When Jesus wept over Jerusalem, the situation did not get better—so it's not the case that, as Christians, we must always expect consolation.

Let's not forget the times, either, when tears flow without any rational cause, when the answer to the question 'Why are you weeping?' is 'I don't know.' Tiredness, hormone imbalance or the heavy cloud of depression may allow no other expression than to cry. We need not be ashamed that we cannot locate a specific reason but we can be comforted by the knowledge that God knows—and cares. He has given us a Saviour who has wept himself and understands our tears.

Some people will say that there is comfort in the scriptures, but getting to know God's purposes through his word may not bring an immediate end to our tears, for they do not deliver us from the situation we are facing. Nevertheless, they can help us to find perspective and encourage us to trust and rely on God's strength, weak as we are.

However wonderful the poetry of scripture, however pertinent the words and God-inspired the prophecies, they will remain mere words unless we seek a personal relationship with Jesus Christ, the Son of God. It is the step that Mary took, early on that fateful morning. She came to the tomb in the darkness—literally and metaphorically—but she ran to tell her news in the light of the new day, the light of her Saviour's resurrection glory.

For reflection

Now the dwelling of God is with human beings, and he will live with them. They will be his people, and God himself will be with them and be their God. He will wipe every tear from their eyes. There will be no more death or mourning or crying or pain, for the old order of things has passed away.

REVELATION 21:3–4

Chapter 20

'Do you love me?'

When they had finished eating, Jesus said to Simon Peter, 'Simon son of John, do you truly love me more than these?' 'Yes, Lord,' he said, 'you know that I love you.' Jesus said, 'Feed my lambs.' Again Jesus said, 'Simon son of John, do you truly love me?' He answered, 'Yes, Lord, you know that I love you.' Jesus said, 'Take care of my sheep.' The third time he said to him, 'Simon son of John, do you love me?' Peter was hurt because Jesus asked him the third time, 'Do you love me?' He said, 'Lord, you know all things; you know that I love you.' Jesus said, 'Feed my sheep.'

JOHN 21:15–17

Chapter 21 is John's great epilogue. Let's consider how the disciple concludes his Gospel with the fundamental themes of forgiveness, renewal and commitment. These themes form the basis of faith for every Christian believer and will need to be revisited time and again through life. First, however, we need to look at the background to the passage.

The events of the previous days—the arrest, trial, crucifixion, burial and resurrection of their master, Jesus—had knocked the disciples sideways. Drained of emotion, bereft of his leadership, they didn't know what to do. Their minds were reeling with what seemed unimaginable—totally impossible—yet they had all been eyewitnesses to a truth that would change the world.

Suddenly Peter, unable to sit around any longer, told the others that he was going fishing. Having to 'do' something is a very familiar response to upheaval, so we can understand Peter's need to head for his fishing boat. Fishing had been his life in this part of

Galilee; it was the comfort zone where he could temporarily blot out his trauma. Evidently the others were only too glad to join him.

Along this stretch of the lake, Jesus had first called the brothers Andrew and Simon and predicted to Simon that he would be called Cephas, or Peter, the 'rock' (John 1:41–42). There were so many special memories for the disciples, but the one uppermost in Peter's mind at this time would no doubt have been his crushing guilt and humiliation after denying Jesus in the high priest's courtyard.

The fishing diversion was a total failure: they were out on the lake all night without a bite. By morning their spirits had sunk to even greater despondency, but then a stranger on the shore told them to cast their net on the right side of the boat. Amazing! They nearly capsized under the weight of the catch. At that moment, the 'disciple whom Jesus loved' (v. 7) recognized the figure on the beach. 'It is the Lord!' he exclaimed. Before anything more could be said or done, Peter was in the water, wading as fast as he could to the waiting Jesus.

On the beach, Peter found a charcoal fire with fish already cooking on it. There was also some bread and Jesus invited the men to bring up some of their catch to barbeque. For miserable, hungry men, this must have been a heartwarming sight, but for Peter it was the smell rather than the sight that pierced to his heart. The Greek word for 'charcoal fire' is used only twice in the whole New Testament—here on the beach with Jesus and previously in the high priest's courtyard where Peter made his adamant denials. Peter had been so enthusiastic in his promises of faithfulness, but he had totally abandoned Jesus when his master had most needed him. How could he meet Jesus' gaze over breakfast? Would there have been awkward silence or conversation?

When they had eaten, Jesus and Peter went for a stroll. At some point, I imagine, they stopped and Jesus turned to look directly at Peter. Jesus did not call him 'Peter', though, but 'Simon'. Was this an intentional return to the fisherman's original name, the name he had used before Jesus said, 'And I tell you that you are Peter, and on this rock I will build my church' (Matthew 16:18)? Over those last momentous days in which he had denied all knowledge of Jesus, poor old Peter hadn't been exactly rock-like: he may have felt more comfortable to hear his Lord calling him Simon.

So Jesus said, 'Simon, son of John, do you love me more than these?' By 'these' we can only guess that Jesus was referring to the other disciples still sprawled by the fire, contemplating their magnificent haul. Alternatively, 'these' may have meant the fishing boats in which Peter had grown to manhood and all that was part of his Galilean home. Could he love Jesus enough to leave these ingredients of his life?

When Peter replied that he did love Jesus, he was given a commission: 'Feed my lambs' (v. 15). In other words, he was asked to care for the weak and vulnerable believers. Next, when Peter affirmed his love the second time, Jesus told him to 'take care of my sheep' (v. 16)—to lead the group and take pastoral responsibility of the followers when Jesus was no longer physically with them.

These deep questions were emotive enough, but Jesus pressed on to ask Peter for the third time, 'Simon, son of John, do you love me?' John recalls that Peter was 'hurt' that Jesus felt it necessary to repeat the question, but let's look at it in the context of rabbinical teaching methods. Something said once could be of great importance, but a threefold repetition gave the words vital significance.

Jesus was not just asking Peter to look after the believers; he was wiping away the memory of Peter's threefold denial. He was lifting the guilt and shame and the recriminations that would have niggled among the disciples, and he was reinstating 'Simon' as 'Peter, the rock', the disciples' new leader.

Peter was a natural leader, and we read his name in the Gospels far more times than the names of any of the other eleven closest followers. Peter was an impetuous, well-intentioned, enthusiastic disciple, yet he was the disciple whose recorded failures have endeared him to millions over the centuries. He found forgiveness, his courage was renewed and he made his commitment by affirming his unswerving love for his Lord.

Like Peter, we make major mistakes, but, just as Peter found forgiveness, there is forgiveness for us, whatever our failings, when we turn back to Jesus in genuine repentance. We remember that Jesus said, 'I have not come to call the righteous, but sinners' (Matthew 9:13). Jesus will always welcome us back and enable us to continue our discipleship. God has given us the gift of free will, so the onus is upon us to decide how we will respond to the voice of Jesus.

We have journeyed a long way since the beginning of this book, when we were looking at the call of the first disciples and considering our first question. We have now come full circle from the shores of Galilee, where it all started with the tentative disciples wanting to know more about this man called Jesus. Their response took them on a journey of faith in which they witnessed first-hand the most incredible miracles that anyone had ever seen. Over and over again, their hearts leapt as Jesus taught and instructed them. His words and actions transformed their lives. His love and acceptance reached beyond anything they had known. Yet their expectations for Jesus' triumph were destroyed as they watched in horror while Jesus died on the cross. Now, most probably, they were still in a haze of joy and disbelief at seeing another resurrection appearance, this time on the shores of the Sea of Galilee where it all began.

In the 20 questions we have looked at, we have also been on a journey covering many spiritual miles. As with any journey, there have been hills and valleys, sunshine and shadows, moments of confidence and periods of emptiness. It's a journey that began with the question 'What do you want?' and I hope that, through these different questions, you have gained a clearer idea of your own discipleship. Have you been able to answer the subsidiary questions: 'What are your immediate needs? What are you looking for in life? What do you want?' If you have come to any conclusions, you may now be ready to enter into the next phase of commitment.

Tuck yourself away in a quiet place and let your imagination take you to that breakfast spot by the shore. Smell the charcoal; feel the warmth of the morning sun; hear the lapping of the water around the fishing boat. Imagine yourself getting up to walk along the water's edge. Gradually you become aware that Jesus is walking beside you. First of all, you walk in silence, but then Jesus stops. He turns and looks directly at you. You can see his face; his words are gentle. He is asking you, 'Do you love me?' What will you say?

Paul wrote to his beloved friends at Ephesus:

I pray that out of his glorious riches he may strengthen you with power through his Spirit in your inner being, so that Christ may dwell in your hearts through faith. And I pray that you, being rooted and established in love, may have power, together with all the saints, to grasp how wide and long and high and deep is the love of Christ, and to know this love that surpasses knowledge—that you may be filled to the measure of all the fullness of God.

EPHESIANS 3:16–21

My own prayer is that you will be so strengthened that you will be able to respond to Jesus with the heartfelt words of Peter: 'Lord, you know all things; you know that I love you.'

Embracing God's World

Prayers for the yearning heart

Joyce Huggett

As we draw closer to God, we begin to share his love and compassion for his creation. And as we listen to the yearning of our hearts and begin to linger in God's presence, we find ourselves joining the Holy Spirit's work of intercession for the people and places of our beautiful but broken world.

This revised edition of a collection first published in 1996 brings together Joyce Huggett's personal selection of prayers new and old, some by contemporary writers, others whose gentle power has been proved over many years of use. *Embracing God's World* can be a bedside aid to personal prayer or a book to resource intercessions and worship in both small groups and the wider church community.

ISBN 978 1 84101 574 3 £7.99
Available from your local Christian bookshop or, in case of difficulty, direct from BRF using the order form on page 119.

Meeting the Saviour

The glory of Jesus in the Gospel of John

Derek Tidball

Just what exactly is so special about Jesus of Nazareth—his teaching, his life, his death, his impact on human beings? John's Gospel has a one-word answer: 'glory', one of the key themes of that Gospel, alongside 'light', 'life' and 'truth'. John's testimony is that as he and his friends watched, listened and shared in the life of the one they knew to be Jesus from Nazareth, the son of Mary and Joseph the carpenter, they saw 'glory' in him and radiating from him.

This book reflects on key stories and teaching in John's Gospel, considering how they portray Jesus' time on earth as in effect one long transfiguration that revealed, to those able and willing to see it, the glory that is the signature of God in creation. And we too are invited to meet the Saviour, allowing ourselves to be transformed by his touch.

ISBN 978 1 84101 497 5   £6.99
Available from your local Christian bookshop or, in case of difficulty, direct from BRF using the order form on page 119.

Living and Praying the Lord's Prayer

Peter Graves

Many of us know the Lord's Prayer so well that we take it for granted, and can even find ourselves saying the words without thinking. In doing so, we undervalue this masterpiece of spirituality, which in less than 60 words gets to the heart of the message of Jesus.

Although a prayer in its own right, the Lord's Prayer also serves as a pattern and framework for our praying, and a way of exploring the very nature of prayer itself. This book will help readers to see it in a new light, and then prayerfully to reflect upon the insights gained from reading it.

ISBN 978 1 84101 182 0 £6.99
Available from your local Christian bookshop or, in case of difficulty, direct from BRF using the order form on page 119.

brf

Resourcing your spiritual journey

through...

- Bible reading notes
- Books for Advent & Lent
- Books for Bible study and prayer
- Books to resource those working with under 11s in school, church and at home

- Quiet days and retreats
- Training for primary teacher and children's leaders
- Godly Play
- Barnabas RE Days

For more information, visit the **brf** website at **www.brf.org.ul**